STOICISM:

The Manual of Ancient Stoic Philosophy as a Way of Modern Life - A Beginner's Guide to Develop Mindset Through Critical Thinking and Self-Discipline, and to Increase Your Wisdom Daily

By: David Drive

Copyright © 2019 – David Drive
All rights reserved

The content contained within this book may not be reproduced, duplicated or transmitted without direct written permission from the author or the publisher.
Under no circumstances will any blame or legal responsibility be held against the publisher, or author, for any damages, reparation, or monetary loss due to the information contained within this book. Either directly or indirectly.

Legal Notice:
This book is copyright protected. This book is only for personal use. You cannot amend, distribute, sell, use, quote or paraphrase any part, or the content within this book, without the consent of the author or publisher.

Disclaimer Notice:
Please note the information contained within this document is for educational and entertainment purposes only. All effort has been executed to present accurate, up to date, and reliable, complete information. No warranties of any kind are declared or implied. Readers acknowledge that the author is not engaging in the rendering of legal, financial, medical or professional advice. The content within this book has been derived from various sources. Please consult a licensed professional before attempting any techniques outlined in this book.

By reading this document, the reader agrees that under no circumstances is the author responsible for any losses, direct or indirect, which are incurred as a result of the use of information contained within this document, including, but not limited to errors, omissions, or inaccuracies.

Table of Contents

Introduction 1

Chapter 1: The Story of Stoicism 4

    Socrates 5

    The Cynics 7

    Zeno of Citium 9

    Chryssipus 10

    Seneca 13

    Epictetus 14

    Stoics vs. Epicureans 16

    Marcus Aurelius 18

    Stoic Revivals 20

    Modern Stoicism 22

Chapter 2: Basics of Stoicism 24

    The Power of Choice 27

    First Impressions 30

    Human Nature 32

    Virtue and Happiness 33

    Indifferent Things 36

Pathos 38

Good Feelings 41

Chapter 3: Critical Thinking 43

Everyday Problems and Stoic Solutions 44

Not Adding Anything.. 60

Chapter 4: Self-Discipline and Resilience 63

The Three Disciplines of Stoicism 65

Twelve Principles of Self-Discipline 68

Control Desire 69

Keep Your Thoughts on the Boat... 70

Remember That Nothing is Free 71

Let Them Laugh 73

Don't Reach for Things.. 74

Play Your Part 75

Avoid Envy 76

Don't Get Carried Away.. 77

Don't Show Off 78

Watch Yourself.. 79

Never Criticize Others 80

Accept Every Criticism 81

Chapter 5: Managing the Emotions 82

    Anxiety 84

    Accidents 85

    Welcome Trouble 86

    Check Your Principles 87

    Hindrances 89

    Insult 90

    Criticism 91

    Mistreatment 92

    Misfortune 94

    Contagious Emotions 95

    Ambition 95

    Difficult People 96

    Illness 97

    Loss 98

    Grief 99

    Depression 100

    Death 101

Chapter 6: Great Stoics and Admirers of Stoicism ... 103

    Political Leaders 104

Military Leaders 107

Entertainers..109

Athletes 112

Authors 115

Business Leaders... 117

Stoicism: Life-Hack or Way of Life?.................................. 119

Chapter 7: Stoicism and Psychology 122

Development of CBT...125

Thoughts, Emotions, and Actions 128

Cognitive Distortions... 131

Stages of Cognitive Behavioral Therapy 134

Stoicism in Positive Psychology..............................135

The Stoic Attitudes and Behaviors Self-Rating Scale...........138

Stoic Habits 140

Chapter 8: Everyday Stoicism............................... 143

Chapter 9: The Stoic Leader................................... 159

The Nine Rules of Stoic Leadership 161

The Advice of the Emperor 163

Conclusion 177

Introduction

"True happiness is to enjoy the present, without anxious dependence upon the future, not to amuse ourselves with either hopes or fears but to rest satisfied with what we have, which is sufficient, for he that is so, wants nothing."

— Seneca

Congratulations on choosing *Stoicism: The Manual of Ancient Stoic Philosophy as a Way of Modern Life*, and thank you for doing so.

The following chapters will discuss the ancient philosophy of Stoicism, which is making a major comeback in the modern world. The philosophy that once guided emperors now helps CEOs, professional coaches, generals, and other leaders. The self-disciplined Stoic way of life is ideal for anyone who wants to overcome difficult or impossible situations and turn problems into advantages. Since ancient times, Stoicism has offered something unique and valuable: the secret to genuine and lasting happiness. The Stoic can meet all of life's ups and downs with untroubled serenity, secure in the knowledge of what truly matters.

This book will tell you everything you need to know about the history of Stoicism and the great Stoic thinkers Epictetus, Seneca, and Marcus Aurelius, as well as the core ideas of Stoicism, the Stoic approach to critical thinking and pragmatism, Stoic methods for building self-discipline and resilience, and methods for handling emotional turmoil with Stoic meditations. It will also tell you how history's greatest leaders and innovators have applied the wisdom of Stoicism and how modern psychology has adopted Stoic principles, with techniques and practices you can apply in your daily life. The book concludes with the advice of the Roman emperor and Stoic Marcus Aurelius on the leadership mindset.

There are many other books on Stoicism on the market, but you chose this one. Thanks again. Every effort was put into the writing of this book to make it as useful as possible. Please enjoy!

Chapter 1: The Story of Stoicism

"Be like a rocky promontory against which the restless surf continually pounds; it stands fast while the churning sea is lulled to sleep at its feet."
— *Marcus Aurelius*

Stoicism is an ancient philosophy and way of life, founded by a man named Zeno of Citium about 2300 years ago. Even though Stoicism is a school of philosophy, it's very different from most of the philosophies you may be familiar with. The Stoics are not remembered for abstract debates or complex theories. Their main focus was on how to live and how to be happy.

In fact, Stoicism claims to hold the secret to happiness. The Stoic approach is counterintuitive, but many people have found it to be both compelling and effective. For thousands of years now, people have been using the insights of the great Stoic philosophers to live better lives. You can do the same by adopting the simple and practical Stoic mindset in your own life. Let's start by finding out more about the history of this remarkable philosophy, which has been guiding leaders and comforting the troubled for more than two millennia.

Socrates

The story of Stoicism begins with Socrates, the most famous and influential of all the ancient philosophers. Socrates himself didn't write any books. He was mostly remembered for having asked penetrating questions about everyday topics. Unfortunately for the philosopher, some people interpreted his persistent questioning as a deliberate attack on traditional values. Socrates was arrested and charged with corrupting the minds of his young students. Condemned to death in 399 BC, Socrates refused to flee the city and faced his execution with calm courage that amazed and impressed even his most bitter critics.

The students of Socrates took up his mantle, including the almost equally influential Plato. Most of what we know about Socrates comes from Plato's writings, including the somewhat extreme idea that virtue is the only real good there is. Socrates seems to have been deeply concerned with the question of what is good, and he often questioned his fellow Athenians about their opinions on the topic. The commonplace answers failed to satisfy him, and Socrates continued to probe the question throughout his life. Eventually, he concluded that our own ethical choices are the key to happiness.

In Plato's *Euthydemus*, Socrates teaches that nothing is truly good or bad except for human actions. The four "cardinal virtues" of wisdom, justice, temperance, and courage are genuinely good, but the random events of human life are neither good nor bad. By refusing to flee when he was condemned to death, Socrates set a powerful example of moral strength that influenced many of the philosophers who came after him.

The Cynics

Socrates's most famous student was certainly Plato, but Plato's mystical tendencies did not appeal to all his fellow disciples. Antisthenes was another student of Socrates who founded an extreme philosophy known as Cynicism, based on the idea that people should reject all social norms and live lives of absolute minimalism, focused exclusively on virtue.

Antisthenes and his followers earned the nickname of "dogs" (ancient Greek *kynikos*) because they lived outside, giving up all material possessions. The most famous Cynic philosopher—a man named Diogenes—lived in a tub in the streets of Athens. When the conqueror Alexander the Great came to visit the famous wise man, the only thing Diogenes would say to him was, "you're blocking my light!"

Cynics like Diogenes considered virtue the only good and rejected everything, from marriage to politics, as useless distractions from the ultimate goal.

Their fellow Greeks found the Cynics both fascinating and shocking at the same time, and they told many anecdotes about the outrageous behavior of Cynics like Diogenes. In one of these tales, Diogenes throws away his only possession—a simple cup—after seeing a child drink water with his bare hands.

Diogenes often acted with startling fearlessness toward the rich and powerful. (Our modern word "cynic" was inspired by his constant sarcastic comments toward the normal citizens of Athens.) Sold into slavery after being captured by pirates, Diogenes was asked what kind of work he could do. "I'm good at leading men," the philosopher replied. "That man over there looks like he needs a leader, sell me to him." With this bold reply, Diogenes secured himself a comfortable position as tutor to a rich man's children.

The Cynics were totally committed to their extreme philosophy, and the best of them did seem to be happier and freer than the average person. However, not many people would be capable of giving up everything and becoming homeless in the pursuit of happiness. Stoicism began with Zeno of Citium, a student of Cynicism who thought the original Cynic teachings went too far.

Zeno of Citium

In Zeno's opinion, the Cynics were right to say that virtue was the only real good. However, he didn't think most people would be able to live the Cynic lifestyle, and he didn't think extreme minimalism was really necessary for either virtue or happiness. By rejecting family, property, and any participation in normal society, the Cynics were treating these things as if they were bad.

The original teaching of Socrates was not that such things are bad, only that they aren't genuinely good. If something is neither good nor bad, then it must be indifferent, and that's exactly what Zeno began to teach. At a marketplace in Athens, known as the "Painted Porch" (*Stoa Poikile*), Zeno taught his students that the secret to happiness was to consider most things to be indifferent but not necessarily to give them up completely like the extremist Cynics.

For example, a follower of Zeno might happen to get married, inherit wealth, or become a political leader. Unlike a Cynic, he wouldn't be expected to reject these opportunities, but he would still be expected to remain indifferent to them, treating them as fundamentally unimportant compared to living a life of wisdom, justice, temperance, and courage.

Because Zeno and his followers met and discussed their ideas at the Painted Porch, they became known as the "Porch" school or "Stoa." Followers of the Stoa were known as Stoics.

Chryssipus

After Zeno died, the second leader of the Stoa was a man named Cleanthes. Cleanthes was succeeded in about 230 BC by the philosopher Chryssipus, who was, for many centuries, the most famous and influential of all the Stoics.

Unlike the later Stoics, such as Epictetus, Chryssipus was interested in many aspects of philosophy other than ethics. Where Epictetus and Marcus Aurelius would write mostly about how to live a good life, Chryssipus developed his own system of logic, his theories about religion and the nature of the universe, and so on.

For example, Stoic logic that was developed by Chryssipus included five types of argument:

If A, then B. A. Therefore, B.

Example: If anyone can be happy without getting married, then marriage is not needed for happiness. Some people are happy without getting married. Therefore, marriage is not needed for happiness.

If A, then B. Not B. Therefore, not A.

Example: If wealth is needed for happiness, all poor people will be unhappy. Not all poor people are unhappy. Therefore, wealth is not needed for happiness.

Not both A and B. A. Therefore, not B.

Example: It cannot be simultaneously true that unhealthy people can be happy and that health is necessary for happiness. Unhealthy people can be happy. Therefore, health is not necessary for happiness.

Either A or B. A. Therefore, not B.

Example: Either power is unnecessary for happiness, or it is necessary. Some people are happy without power. Therefore, power is not necessary for happiness.

Either A or B. Not A. Therefore, B.

Example: Either a good reputation is needed for happiness, or a good reputation is not needed for happiness. Some people are happy without a good reputation. Therefore, a good reputation is not needed for happiness.

As you can see, Stoic logic can be used to produce ethical arguments. These arguments would become the centerpiece of Stoic philosophy.

Seneca

The original Stoa was centered in Athens, but growing Roman influence over Greece eventually resulted in a Stoic diaspora. Stoic teachers left Athens and scattered all over the territories of the Roman Republic until the original Stoa in Athens faded from history.

Stoicism was a popular philosophy among the stern and self-disciplined Roman elite, especially to those like Cato the Younger, who resisted the rise of the dictator Julius Caesar. Cato committed suicide rather than accept Caesar's rule—one of several events that made Stoicism a suspect philosophy in the eyes of some Roman rulers. After all, Stoics taught that virtue was the only *real good*, and that's not a stance any Caesar follower was likely to approve.

After the Roman Republic became the Roman Empire under Caesar Augustus, Stoicism's place in Roman life was somewhat precarious. The Stoic teacher Seneca was sent into exile by the emperor Claudius in 41 AD, only to become the chief advisor to the emperor Nero in 54 AD. When the cruel and corrupt Nero suspected Seneca of joining a plot to assassinate him, he ordered the Stoic teacher to commit suicide. In keeping with Stoic principles, Seneca faced his death with self-disciplined courage.

Seneca is most remembered today for his Epistles or letters to his friend and student Lucilius. It included 124 essays on issues, such as how to face the fear of death or deal with minor daily irritations like excessive noise. He is also believed to be the first ancient writer to question the morality of the Gladiatorial games openly. Seneca is somewhat controversial for his role in Nero's government, but it is generally agreed that he did his best to provide a stabilizing influence before the tyrant turned on him.

Epictetus

Unlike the wealthy and politically connected Seneca, the great Stoic Epictetus came from the lowest levels of Roman society. Born in 55 AD, the future philosopher was a slave to Nero's secretary Epaphroditus. Even his name refers to the fact that he was a slave: Epictetus means "something acquired."

Despite his status as a slave, Epictetus was able to study under the Stoic teacher Musonius Rufus, who taught a simple and pragmatic version of Stoicism that emphasized practical questions of daily life rather than the other topics that had fascinated Chryssipus. When Epictetus began to teach, he kept the same focus on practical issues.

Freed by Epaphroditus, Epictetus was forced to go into exile when the emperor Domitian decided to persecute the Stoics. During his exile in Greece, Epictetus taught his wealthy students how to make better decisions and live better lives, often referring to them sarcastically as "slaves" because of their inability to control their own emotions.

Epictetus never wrote a book of his own, but his student Arrian took extensive notes in class and later published these as a series of books: the four-volume *Discourses* and the *Enchiridion* or "Handbook." These books proved to be hugely popular and influential, to the extent that people interested in Stoicism would study Epictetus rather than earlier Stoic works by Zeno or Chryssipus. As a result, none of the works of these early Stoics have been preserved.

It's not that Epictetus taught anything the earlier Stoics would have disagreed with, but he focused exclusively on practical advice and left the speculations to other philosophers. Most readers preferred the simple and practical life advice of Epictetus to abstract ideas about the universe, and that's what Stoicism is now remembered for. Stoic logic and Stoic physics are now known only to professors of philosophy, but the Stoic way of life has continued to guide and inspire people for thousands of years.

Stoics vs. Epicureans

The Stoics were rivals of the Epicureans, a school that believed pleasure to be the only good and pain the only evil. To the self-disciplined Stoics, this teaching must have seemed like amoral and self-serving hedonism. In reality, Epicurus taught a much more balanced way of life than his basic doctrine might suggest.

Although Epicurus believed that pleasure was the only good, he acknowledged that many pleasures lead to pain later. For example, the pleasure of eating sugary or fatty food can lead to the pain of tooth decay or other health problems. The pleasure of sex can lead to the pain of broken relationships or venereal diseases. Any pleasure to be gained from antisocial or criminal behavior would be tainted by the pain of anxiety about possible consequences.

To avoid the pain that can come from pleasure, Epicurus taught a simple and dignified lifestyle based on enjoying good food and conversation in moderation with a handful of chosen friends. Epictetus himself could hardly have objected to this sort of life, as Stoics consider friends, good food, and conversation to be pleasant things despite being "indifferent."

Despite the inoffensive nature of the Epicurean lifestyle, Epictetus often attacked the doctrine in his lectures. If pleasure is the only real good, and pain is the only real evil, then the Stoic approach to happiness has no foundation. Because he believed from his own experience as a slave that happiness has nothing to do with pleasure or pain, Epictetus did everything he could to defeat the arguments of the Epicureans. The irony of the dispute between the two schools is that they advocated similar lifestyles for completely opposite reasons.

Marcus Aurelius

Stoicism helped Epictetus endure the sufferings of a slave, but it also helped Marcus Aurelius endure the very different problems of a Roman emperor. Adopted by his uncle Antoninus Pius, Marcus became the heir to the throne when his uncle was declared emperor in 138 AD.

Although emperors, such as Vespasian and Domitian, had suppressed the philosophers, Antoninus Pius provided financial support for teachers of philosophy. His heir Marcus Aurelius was deeply affected by his study of Stoicism, and he drew comfort from the philosophy when he became emperor in 161.

During Marcus's reign, the Roman Empire faced a series of wars with Germanic tribes, such as the Marcomanni and the Quadi, as well as the Sarmatians, the Parthian Empire, and the Kingdom of Armenia. With so many enemies, the emperor was away from home on a campaign for years at a stretch, traveling with the army rather than governing from Rome.

From an army camp in the land of the Quadi, Marcus Aurelius began to keep a kind of diary, encouraging himself to face the challenges of war and leadership with a Stoic mindset. The tone of this diary is highly personal, and the emperor does not seem to have intended for other people to read it ever. Many passages are simple reminders not to get irritated with other people or not to fear death, a bad reputation, or poor health:

"What if someone despises me? Let me see to it. But I will see to it that I won't be found doing or saying anything contemptible. What if someone hates me? Let me see to that. But I will see to it that I'm kind and good-natured to all and prepared to show even the hater where they went wrong—not in a critical way or show off my patience but genuinely and usefully."

A real "philosopher king," Marcus Aurelius seems to have made every effort to govern the Roman Empire with justice and wisdom.

The diary was more of a spiritual exercise than a work of philosophy, but someone preserved it and passed it down under the name *Meditations*, and it is now at least as influential as the works of Epictetus. Despite the earlier fame of the men who founded and led the original Stoa, the much later and more personal works of the emperor and the slave now define Stoicism for most people.

Stoic Revivals

The influence of Stoicism eventually declined, but Stoic ideas were absorbed into later philosophies such as Neoplatonism. The Roman Empire turned away from pagan philosophy to embrace the new religion of Christianity, and the center of the empire switched from Rome to Byzantium. By the time the last emperor of Rome was deposed in 476 AD, Stoicism no longer existed as a distinct school of philosophy.

The influence of Stoic values can be seen in the work of Boethius, a man who could be described as the last of the classical philosophers. A Roman in the service of Theodoric the Great, the King of the Ostrogoths, Boethius was arrested and condemned to death in 524 for plotting against Rome's Germanic rulers. While awaiting his execution, Boethius composed a work called *The Consolation of Philosophy*, with lines that could have been written by Epictetus or Marcus Aurelius centuries earlier:

"Nothing is miserable unless you think it so; and on the other hand, nothing brings happiness unless you are content with it."

The Consolation of Philosophy was a popular work in medieval Europe, but the Catholic Church was somewhat skeptical of what was originally a pagan way of life. However, the Stoic emphasis on virtue and self-discipline seemed perfectly acceptable to many Christians, and some monasteries even used an edited version of Epictetus's *Handbook* as a guide for monks.

The *Meditations* of Marcus Aurelius were known to a few scholars and churchmen but were not widely available until the Renaissance. Around the same time that the *Meditations* became available to the reading public, a philosopher named Justus Lipsius made a determined attempt to create a new and Christianized form of Stoicism. In his *De Constantia* of 1584, Lipsius argued that Stoic teachings could be useful for Christians facing hard times. Lipsius was criticized harshly by some religious leaders for his attempt to revive Stoicism, but philosophers like Montaigne and Spinoza adopted elements of Stoic teachings into their own systems. Immanuel Kant's theory of ethics can be traced to the influence of Epictetus.

Modern Stoicism

> "No longer talk at all about the kind of man that a good man ought to be, but be such."
> - Marcus Aurelius

Stoicism is now experiencing its greatest revival since ancient times, with philosophers and self-help writers like Donald Robertson, Ryan Holliday, John Sellars, Lawrence Becker, and William Irvine—all championing a modernized version of the ancient philosophy. The "Stoicism Today" blog offers daily guidance for modern Stoics, and social media sites, like Facebook, have active groups for Stoic practitioners. Mental health counselors also use Stoic ideas in a modified form in Cognitive Behavioral Therapy and other treatments.

Much like Epictetus and Marcus Aurelius, today's Stoics emphasize practical questions of daily living rather than abstract ideas. Stoicism has always claimed to offer the secret to happiness, and many people are intrigued enough to want to try it for themselves.

Chapter 2: Basics of Stoicism

"Freedom is the only worthy goal in life. It is won by disregarding things that lie beyond our control."

- Epictetus

The basic principle of Stoicism is that some things are under your control, and some things are not. According to the great Stoic philosophers like Epictetus and Marcus Aurelius, the main cause of unhappiness is confusing things that are not under your control for things that are. When you seek happiness in things you can't control, you suffer from anxiety and stress. When you seek happiness only in things you really do control, you are totally free.

If this seems like a simple insight, that's because it is. You don't have to understand any abstract metaphysical ideas to get the point of Stoicism. All you have to do is accept and try to live by this one simple idea. Whatever is not under your control is not worth worrying about. Only the things that are under your control should concern you at all.

Epictetus gives four examples of things that are not under your control–your body, your property, your reputation, and the amount of authority you have over others. These are only examples, but they do cover many of the problems people run into in life.

If there's one thing most of us assume we have control over, it's our own body. Epictetus invites us to ask ourselves whether this control is real or an illusion. Can you guarantee that you'll never suffer from illness or injury? Can you keep your body from aging? Nobody can. In the most extreme circumstances, you might no longer be able to move at all. Your body is something you do not control.

The same is true of your property. "A man's home is his castle," as people say, but you can lose that home to a foreclosure or bankruptcy. Your car can be stolen. Your building can burn down. As much as you might want to, you don't control your own property.

Reputation is another example. No matter how hard you work to build up your business, anonymous social media reviews can do a lot of damage to your reputation. The same is true for your private life. You might think of yourself as a good and honest person, but you can't control what other people think of you.

Authority, or "command" as Epictetus calls it, is beyond your control as well. Your ability to command other people depends on two things—your role in whatever organization you work for and the willingness or ability of your subordinates to do whatever you ask of them. If you're not in a position of authority, you cannot command others. Even if you are, you cannot be sure they will choose to obey you. If they do obey you, you cannot be sure they will do a good job.

Think about how you would feel if you became seriously ill, if you lost your home to bankruptcy, if other people saw you as a bad person, or if you could never get other people to do what you wanted them to do. If you're like most people, you would feel unhappy if any of these things happened—yet you have no power to keep them from happening.

Epictetus tells us that we cannot be free and that we can never be truly happy, as long as our happiness depends on things we cannot control. Because we cannot control our bodies, our property, our reputations, or our ability to command others, we should think of all these things as irrelevant to our happiness.

The Power of Choice

If we have no control over our bodies, our property, our reputation, or our ability to command others, then what do we have control over? According to Epictetus:

"Things in our control are opinion, pursuit, desire, aversion, and, in a word, whatever are our own actions."

You control your opinions because you're the one who decides whether you agree with something or not. You control what you pursue in life and what you don't. For example, you can decide whether to go to college or accept a marriage proposal, among other things. You control what you avoid, for instance, by not eating certain foods when you're on a diet. Your own actions are under your control, and anything other than your own actions is not under your control.

According to the Stoics, the cause of unhappiness is simple confusion. When you mistake something that isn't under your control for something that is, you chain your happiness to something that can be taken away from you at any time. The inevitable result is that you suffer whether you get what you want or not.

For example, you might think you'll be happy if you find a romantic partner, but as soon as you do meet someone, you start feeling anxious about losing that person. You might think you'll be happy about getting that promotion to management, but you end up feeling stressed out because your subordinates aren't as motivated or competent as you are. The source of stress, anxiety, and other negative emotions is the desire to control things that were never yours to control in the first place.

As Epictetus says:

"The things in our control are, by nature, free, unrestrained, unhindered; but those not in our control are weak, slavish, restrained, and belonging to others. Remember, then, that if you suppose that things which are slavish by nature are also free and that what belongs to others is your own, then you will be hindered. You will lament, you will be disturbed, and you will find fault both with gods and men."

So, how can you free yourself from this self-defeating tendency? In the philosophy of Stoicism, the key to genuine and lasting happiness is your own ability to recognize the difference between things you control and things you don't. If you can learn to tell the difference, you will find true freedom and true happiness.

First Impressions

There's a difference between an instinctive reaction and the type of thinking that leads to unhappiness. If you stubbed your toe, your natural reaction would be to cry out in pain. That's an instinctive response and not one that most Stoics would criticize (despite the popular use of the word "stoic" to mean a person who doesn't openly react to pain or discomfort). On the other hand, if you start telling yourself that you are having an awful day because you stubbed your toe, or if you start saying things like "why does this always happen to me," you've gone beyond the instinctive reaction and assented to the idea that stubbing your toe is "bad" and can make you unhappy.

Because you cannot do anything to guarantee that you will never stub your toe again, you've given away your control over your own happiness. The Stoics taught that we should always be careful about what we assent to, so we don't let false judgments about life ruin our happiness.

When anything happens, Epictetus says that you should avoid the impulse to classify it as good or bad immediately. Instead, you should remind yourself that your first impression may not be accurate. Whatever is causing the impression may or may not be essential to your happiness, and you don't want to make an assumption before you understand what type of thing you're dealing with. Taking a step back from your first impression, ask yourself whether this thing is under your control or not. Can it be taken away from you without your consent? If it isn't under your control, be ready to say, "this is nothing to me."

By taking this counterintuitive and radical step, you can free yourself from dependence on things that can be taken away from you, allowing you to center your happiness on things that no one can take away from you. You can apply this in situations as simple as a stubbed toe by reminding yourself that the pain is an instinctive and natural reaction but that it cannot have any effect on your happiness. You can even apply it in much more drastic situations, such as the famous example of Epictetus and his master. When Epictetus was still a slave, his cruel master deliberately broke his leg just to prove to him that he could not use Stoicism to control his emotions. By remaining calm and imperturbable, Epictetus proved that he did have that power, a demonstration that won him his freedom.

Human Nature

The Stoics considered nature to be the ultimate guide for human behavior, so why did they teach people to disregard perfectly natural emotions? To understand this particular aspect of the Stoic philosophy, we need to consider what type of nature we share with all other creatures and what type of nature is uniquely human.

Hunger is something we share with all other living beings. You could say that it's part of our shared animal nature. When a cat feels hungry, it will always eat if it has food in its bowl. A hungry wolf will always hunt, and a hungry cow will always chew grass. A hungry person will usually eat if given the opportunity, but there are situations when people choose not to eat.

For instance, a person might choose not to eat because the only available food is unhealthy or because it's against a special diet they've decided to follow.

People sometimes fast for religious reasons or choose not to eat just to make a point, as in a hunger strike. While hunger is part of our shared animal nature, the ability to choose whether to eat or not is uniquely human.

This faculty of choice—what the Stoics called the "ruling faculty"—is our human nature, which we don't share with other animals. A horse that did not act like a horse would strike us as something unnatural. According to the Stoics, a human who fails to exercise the ruling faculty is equally unnatural.

Because we have the natural ability to make rational choices, we cannot fulfill our nature as human beings unless we make full use of that ability. While it might be natural for a dog to gobble up all the available food even if it makes him feel sick later, it's more natural for a human to exercise restraint and avoid getting sick.

Virtue and Happiness

The ability to make rational choices is what the Stoics called "virtue," and they considered it the secret to happiness. The happiest life for a lion is to live like a lion, and the happiest life for a human being is to live like a human being. Since the one thing that sets us apart from other creatures is our ability to make rational choices, the use of that ability is the one thing we need to be truly happy. Thus, virtue and happiness are the same things to the Stoics.

There was a lot of disagreement among the ancient Greek philosophers about the nature of happiness and the best way to achieve it. Almost all the ancient Greek schools of philosophy taught that no one could be happy without living a virtuous life, but they disagreed on how central virtue was to overall happiness.

For the followers of Aristotle, happiness was a combination of virtue and what we would think of as good fortune—if you were reasonably wealthy, healthy, good-looking, and virtuous, then they would say you were happy.

For the followers of Epicurus, virtue was mostly a simple matter of increasing the pleasure in your life while reducing the pain. The main reason to be virtuous, according to Epicureans, was to avoid all the stress and anxiety caused by making bad decisions.

The Stoics disagreed vehemently with both positions. If happiness depends on wealth, health, and good looks, then most people have little chance of ever being happy. The Stoics were interested in finding a way of life that could bring happiness for anyone who practiced it, regardless of life circumstances. If happiness is just a matter of experiencing as much pleasure as possible and as little pain as possible, then virtue really has little to do with it. The Stoics wanted people to be both happy and good so that happiness would be something much better than mere pleasure.

To the Stoics, the other schools of Greek philosophy sought only a partial and dependent sort of happiness, a happiness that could be lost just as easily as it was gained. They wanted more, but they also wanted it to be available to everyone.

That's why the Stoics taught a different and much more unusual doctrine—true happiness and virtue are the same things, allowing a person to be perfectly happy regardless of circumstances.

If you're happy, regardless of circumstances, you don't need wealth or authority or a good reputation. You don't even need health, which most people think of as a bare minimum for happiness. You have everything you need, and you can never lose it. As long as you're exercising your ruling faculty, everything else is indifferent.

Indifferent Things

Most people would describe health, wealth, a positive reputation, and authority as "good" to have, and most people would describe the opposites of all those things as "bad." According to the Stoics, none of those things are either good or bad because none of them can cause you to be happy or unhappy on their own. No one wants to be sick, but there are sick people who feel happy and healthy people who feel unhappy. No one wants to be poor, but there are poor people who feel happy and rich people who feel unhappy.

If none of these things are either good or bad, then they can only be indifferent, and that's exactly what the Stoics called them. Anything not under your own control is referred to in Stoicism as indifferent to emphasize that it isn't something essential for happiness.

It is still the case that no one would intentionally choose to be unhealthy or poor or to have a bad reputation. Even though being wealthy isn't really good, it's perfectly natural to prefer wealth to poverty. Even though being sick isn't really bad, it's also natural to try to avoid sickness.

In the Stoic philosophy, it's fine to prefer some things to others, as long as you remember that they are still "indifferent," meaning they aren't essential for your own or anyone else's happiness. Since they aren't essential, you can be happy whether you have them or not.

The one thing Stoics consider essential to happiness is the skillful and rational use of the ruling faculty or in one word, "virtue." Stoic virtue includes all the traditional virtues, such as courage, temperance, justice, and wisdom, but it defines all of them as the simple use of rational choice.

For example, if you hear a child crying for help from inside a burning building, your first impression might be that the flames are terrifying, even though you would like to save the child. A Stoic would have the same first impression but would rationally conclude that death is not actually bad and that people have a duty to help and protect each other, wherever possible. This would lead the Stoic to act with courage and save the child.

Less dramatically, a Stoic might be just as tempted as anyone else by a decadent breakfast buffet but would rationally decide to eat with temperance and preserve his health. A Stoic might be tempted to feel angry by an irritating neighbor but would act with wisdom and justice rather than giving in to the anger instinct.

In every case, the Stoic uses our uniquely human power of choice (or "ruling faculty") to make rational and virtuous decisions rather than get carried away by emotional first impressions. Freed from the fear and anxiety caused by false judgments, the Stoic is happy, no matter what happens.

Pathos

If Stoics are happy by definition, why do we use the word "stoic" to describe people who don't seem to display any emotion? It's not that the Stoic is covering up all the painful emotions. That wouldn't be happy at all. Instead, the Stoic is free from certain types of emotion that cause unnecessary suffering.

In modern English, the word "pathos" refers to a feeling of sadness or pity in a movie or a book. If you find yourself feeling sorry for one of the characters, that scene has pathos in it. The word "pathos" comes from ancient Greek, and the Stoics used it to refer to the emotions that cause people to feel sorry for themselves.

For example, if your stocks suddenly increased in value, you'd probably feel delighted. If the stock market crashed, you'd probably feel depressed and upset. The value of your stocks is not under your control, so your delight in one situation is basically the cause of your distress in the other situation. To an ancient Stoic thinker named Zeno of Citium, Delight and Distress are both *pathê* or types of pathos.

If you started dating someone you found very attractive, you'd probably feel desire. If they stopped returning your calls and texts, you might feel fear. Whether someone wants to date you or not is not under your control, so your desire in one situation causes your fear in the other situation. Desire and Fear are also types of pathos.

In these pairs, a seemingly good emotion is paired with a seemingly bad emotion: Delight with Distress and Desire with Fear.

"GOOD"	"BAD"
Delight	Distress
Desire	Fear

These emotions can also be categorized by when they happen in time. Delight refers to the present and Desire to the future because Desire is the anticipation of a future Delight. Distress refers to the present and Fear to the future because Fear is the anticipation of future Distress.

PRESENT	FUTURE
Delight	Desire
Distress	Fear

These four *pathê* or "passions" are all causes of suffering.

Delight and Desire might both seem pleasant, but because they aren't under your control, they can't actually be "good." Mistaking them for genuine good only leads to suffering and anxiety. Distress and Fear both seem unpleasant, but because they aren't under your control, they can't actually be "bad." Thinking of them as genuinely bad leads to suffering and anxiety.

None of the four Passions are good or bad in and of themselves. They only become good or bad because of the false beliefs people hold about them, leading people to invest all their hopes for happiness in aspects of life they cannot control.

Good Feelings

The goal of Stoic practice is *apatheia*, which means to be "without pathos." Although this sounds like "apathy" and is the origin of the word, the original meaning of *apatheia* is to be free of painful emotions, not all emotions. Instead of pathos, the Stoic experiences "good feelings" or *eupatheiai*. A "good feeling" in the Stoic sense is one that nobody and nothing can take away from you because it is based on things that are under your control.

The Stoics acknowledged three *eupatheiai*: Joy, Caution, and Wishing. The three good feelings have something in common with the four types of pathos.

However, unlike the violent passions of Delight, Desire, Distress, and Fear, the three good feelings are calm and tranquil. Joy is the calm and serene enjoyment of something you prefer, without the irrational attachment associated with pathos. Caution is the rational and dignified self-control, with which the Stoic meets danger or makes decisions about her health, without the pathos of irrational fear. Wishing is the reasonable anticipation of a future Joy, without the grasping quality of irrational Desire.

PATHOS	GOOD FEELING
Delight	Joy
Fear	Caution
Desire	Wishing

As you can see, the good feelings of a Stoic are much like those of a regular person, with one big difference. The Stoic is calmly happy under all conditions, while the regular person constantly struggles with negative feelings. By centering your happiness in your own decisions, you can experience the good feelings of Stoicism while avoiding the emotional storms of pathos.

Chapter 3: Critical Thinking

"Very little is needed to make a happy life; it is all within yourself, in your way of thinking."
— Marcus Aurelius

Critical thinking is the core of Stoicism. Whenever anything happens, Stoicism teaches us to step back and question it. Is this situation under my control or not? If it is under my control, the only thing I need to do is make the rational choice—to act with justice and dignity. If it's not under my control, then I need to be ready to say, "this is nothing to me."

Both Epictetus and Marcus Aurelius often taught through examples, brief stories that illustrated Stoic principles. We may not live in ancient Greece or Rome, but the basics of life don't really change. As Marcus Aurelius points out, people acted more or less the same way a hundred years ago and will act more or less the same way a hundred years from now. With a little imagination, most of their examples can be applied to common daily situations in the modern world.

Everyday Problems and Stoic Solutions

Situation: Your wallet gets stolen with all your credit cards.

Solution: Think of it as a trade. You can gain something more valuable than any wallet.

Anytime something upsetting happens, it's an opportunity. From the Stoic viewpoint, an upsetting incident is a chance to practice. Ryan Holiday's Stoic self-help book *The Obstacle is the Way* is based on this simple insight. When something causes you a problem, you can turn it into a chance to become more serene and tranquil.

If you succeed, you'll get something much more valuable than whatever you lost. As Epictetus says, you should never trade something more valuable for something less valuable.

When something goes missing, especially something you use every day, the immediate temptation is to get upset. Most people would, and no one would blame you. Losing your wallet is a hassle, especially when you have to cancel all your credit cards. On the other hand, getting upset won't bring your wallet back. It won't keep you from having to cancel your cards. It won't do anything at all, except to add emotional distress to your other problems.

The prize Stoicism aims at is genuine freedom, and that's worth more than anything else. If your wallet gets stolen, you probably won't be able to help your instinctive reaction of irritation and stress. That's just an impression, but whether you assent to the impression is up to you. If you can succeed in remaining tranquil, you'll make real progress toward your own freedom.

Since freedom is worth so much more than your wallet, you can think of the theft as a successful trade. You're giving up something less valuable (the wallet) for something more valuable (your emotional freedom). It wouldn't make any sense to do the opposite, because you'd be giving up the more valuable item in exchange for the less valuable item. If you lose your wallet and get upset, you lose both the less valuable item and the more valuable item at the same time!

According to Epictetus, it's especially important to pay attention to minor irritations like these. If a ship captain lets his mind wander in a dangerous storm, the ship can go off course and hit the rocks. Daily life is like that storm, and minor irritations like losing your wallet can be enough for you to lose your way.

Situation: You can't stop thinking about getting away on vacation, perhaps to a beach house or some other relaxing place.

Solution: If it's not in your power to get away right now, seek inner peace instead. That's always available.

Marcus Aurelius, the Stoic emperor, must have occasionally wished he could get away more often. He spent much of his career along the borders of the empire, in a series of campaigns against the enemies of Rome. Despite being the emperor, he couldn't get access to new books in the remote military camps where he spent much of his time. He mentions wanting to escape his responsibilities by taking a trip to the country or perhaps to the sea or the mountains.

This sort of yearning is a pathos, specifically the pathos of Desire. Rather than "assenting" to that first impression, Marcus Aurelius reminds himself that he can get away anytime he wants. All he has to do is retreat within, to the calm tranquility of the Stoic mindset. By keeping his inner self secure from turmoil, the Stoic maintains an inner sanctuary. Unlike a vacation home or a resort hotel, this inner sanctuary cannot be taken away.

Even if you do have the opportunity to get away, the pleasant experiences you'll have on vacation are all external. It's fine to prefer them, but they can never match the deep peace that is always available to the inner self.

Situation: You're annoyed by a difference of opinion.

Solution: Remember that the person you disagree with is doing the same thing you are.

Differences in opinion cause a lot of conflicts, especially between family and friends. Perhaps someone in your life supports a candidate you don't like, goes to a church other than your own, hates your favorite band, or roots for a rival sports team. Some of these examples are fairly trivial, but that doesn't stop them from causing problems. People have fallen out for a lot less!

You may have a good and well-reasoned argument for your position, but the person you disagree with may have arguments of their own. Even if the other person's position is based on nothing at all, their opinions are not under your control. If the two of you argue with each other because of your difference of opinion, both of you are doing the same thing.

Epictetus once met a local politician who got offended when people didn't like his favorite actor. As Epictetus pointed out, their attitude wasn't really any different from his. He liked the actor, and they disliked him. Both opinions were equally partisan. He could hardly blame them for booing the actor when he ordered his slaves to cheer the same man. Differences of opinion are differences of viewpoint, and irrational attachment to one side is much the same as an irrational attachment to the other.

Situation: You're upset with the lack of ethics of a coworker.

Solution: Ask yourself whether it's possible for unethical people not to exist.

If you always work hard and do the best job you can, it can be intensely frustrating to work with someone who doesn't share your values. The coworker who doesn't show up on time or do his fair share of work, the coworker who takes credit for others' efforts, and the coworker who steals are all irritating.

As frustrating as it is to work with someone like this, unethical people are here to stay. According to Marcus Aurelius, whenever you find yourself offended at a person's shameless behavior, you should ask yourself a question. Is it possible for the shameless people in the world not to exist?

It doesn't sound very likely, does it? Shameless people have always existed, and in all likelihood, they always will. If shameless people must exist, then expecting never to meet one is expecting the impossible. Expecting the impossible would be the opposite of Stoicism since it would mean wishing for something beyond your control.

The Stoics borrowed some of their ideas from the great philosopher Socrates, who taught that evil was really a form of ignorance. People do things the wrong way because they don't know better and because they have mistaken ideas about what's really good. Expecting someone to do something they don't know would not be reasonable.

No matter what your coworker does, they can never hurt you. Their unethical actions are theirs alone and are not under your control. When a coworker is unethical, you should simply remind yourself that such people exist. Since such people exist in the world, it isn't strange that you happen to work with one.

According to Marcus Aurelius, this realization will naturally cause you to become more kind and patient toward anyone who does things wrong. You don't have to agree with what they do, and you don't have to approve. Just by thinking of them as "uninstructed," you will stop feeling stressed out and irritable. You will remain free.

Situation: Your old friends don't understand why you want to make changes in your life.

Solution: Ask yourself what's most important to you, and act accordingly.

This situation comes up often, especially for people who are trying to get over an addiction or give up a bad habit. If your friends and loved ones are not ready to change, they aren't likely to be supportive when you try to do so. They may even try to drag you down because they don't want things to change between you. Everyone who has ever tried to quit drinking or smoking has had this experience, where friends try to talk you into having "just one" and make it much harder for you to quit successfully.

That's the most obvious example, but there are others. Anytime you try to stop doing something that other people are doing, they're likely to take it as a personal criticism and would encourage you to backslide. It could even be as simple as someone urging you to "stand up for yourself" and get mad about some minor irritation because they don't understand or accept your interest in Stoicism.

As Epictetus says, you can't quit drinking and still be seen as the life of the party because those goals are incompatible. You can't be known for your crushing put-downs and cultivate Stoic tranquility at the same time because those goals are incompatible. So, which is really more important? Which one offers you more benefits? Which one can you commit?

If you really feel that the approval of your friends is the most important thing, then pursue their approval and forget about Stoicism. If you try Stoicism half-heartedly, you'll irritate your friends without gaining tranquility. If you think it's more important to be truly happy, then pursue that completely, and forget about the approval of others. Either way, ask yourself what's truly important and then live by that decision. Not everyone will understand it, but that's not a problem. Their opinions are not under your control, so they aren't essential for your happiness.

Situation: Your child is badly ill.

Solution: Focus on helping your child rather than on your fears.

Epictetus once had a conversation with an unhappy family man, who was filled with anxiety because his child was sick. We don't know exactly the sickness of the child, but in ancient times, it wasn't at all uncommon for people to die in childhood because of illnesses. Knowing this fact, we can assume that the man was deeply worried. He told Epictetus that he was miserable, and the philosopher pointed out that people don't usually marry and have children so they can be miserable.

"I can't help it," said the man. "My daughter is sick."

"If your daughter is sick, then why aren't you at home?" asked Epictetus.

"Seeing her suffer was so upsetting to me that I couldn't stay in the house anymore," the man replied. "I told my wife to send me a message when my daughter gets better."

"Do you think you handled the situation well?" asked Epictetus.

"Whether I handled it well or not, I think my reaction was understandable," said the man. "I love her too much to watch her suffer like that."

"Do you think her mother loves her any less?" asked Epictetus, pointing out the flaw in the man's thinking. If he left the house because of love, then why didn't the girl's mother leave as well? If love causes people to leave you when you need them the most, then what good is it in the first place?

It wasn't "love" that caused the man to leave his sick daughter, but the pathos of Fear. By mistaking his child's illness for something "bad," he left her to suffer alone. The girl's mother knew better and focused on helping her daughter rather than her own emotions.

This example shows the difference between two kinds of love. When love is based on intense emotions, it can easily lead you to harm the person you love. According to Epictetus, that isn't love in the first place. Stoic love is a choice and is always based on doing what's right.

Situation: You're worried about your legacy.

Solution: Remember that everything ends.

As an emperor and an author, Marcus Aurelius must have worried sometimes about how he would be remembered. Would people speak of him as wise and just or as a foolish bookworm who wasted his time on philosophy? If anyone ever read his diary, would they preserve it for future readers or throw it away as useless scrap?

As a practicing Stoic, Marcus Aurelius knew not to get too caught up in this sort of question. Even if people do remember you, those who remember you will die soon enough. If they pass down their respect for you to the next generation, those people will soon die as well. Even if you are remembered for a thousand generations, the last people who remember you will eventually die.

Of course, we now know that Marcus Aurelius is remembered as one of the greatest of the Roman emperors and that his book is considered a classic of philosophy. If he were here today, he'd be the first to remind us that these things are temporary. No matter how long it takes, the day will come when no one remembers him.

Everything ends, and that's just a fact. Whether people remember you or not is not under your control and can't possibly be bad or good. The opinions of others are not worth worrying about.

Situation: Your boss wants you to lie rather than present information that would put him in a bad light.

Solution: Ask yourself which aspect of the situation is under your control. Can your boss do anything to harm you? Would it harm you to lie?

Sometimes, we find ourselves under pressure to do something we know is wrong or beneath our dignity. Epictetus gives the example of a man named Florus, who was trying to decide whether to participate in the degrading spectacles of the tyrant emperor Nero. Agrippinus told him to go ahead, which confused Florus because he knew that Agrippinus had never attended the spectacles himself.

"Why are you saying I should go to the spectacles when you don't go to them?" asked Florus.

"Because I've never even considered going to them," was the reply.

Once you start to debate with yourself about whether or not to give in to pressure, you've already assented to the idea that something external is more important than doing what you know is right. Having made that false judgment, it will be very difficult to avoid doing wrong.

Imagine a boss who asks you to lie at an important meeting rather than present a report unfavorable to him. Your boss has the power to write a bad performance review or maybe get you fired. Does this mean your boss can harm you? No, it does not. Your boss's actions are not under your control, so they can neither harm nor help you. The only thing that could harm you would be to do something wrong.

According to Epictetus, your attitude in this situation should be like that of the Roman senator Priscus, who refused to be a yes-man at the emperor's request: "If you don't ask my opinion, I won't say anything at all. If you do ask my opinion, I have to tell the truth as I see it."

It's not that Epictetus didn't understand the pressures involved. As he says in his Discourses, pleasure is preferable to pain. Keeping your job is preferable to losing your job. Despite these obvious facts, you can never hope to be more than an ordinary person if you do something you know is wrong just to avoid an unpleasant consequence. The person who is aiming for something more will never settle for less and will never even consider trading what is truly important for what is not.

Situation: You're involved in a lawsuit.

Solution: Remember that all actions are caused by opinions.

Epictetus once spoke with a man on his way to Rome to argue a case in court. The journey was a long one, and the man risked everything from discomfort and loss of position to accidental death along the road. When Epictetus asked him why he was going, the man replied that he "had to."

"What makes you say that?" said Epictetus. "It's just an opinion, but it's enough to make you face all these dangers and inconveniences. Everything you do is because of your opinions, and that's equally true of your opponent in this case."

If you're involved in a lawsuit, it's easy to feel that your actions are fixed: the opponent does this, so you do that. The opponent makes this argument, so you make that argument. Even if you firmly believe that your arguments are correct, the opponent probably feels the same way about their own arguments. It's all opinion, just as every action is caused by opinion.

In the Stoic philosophy, the important point is not to win the lawsuit but to make sure that your own opinions are not mistaken. It would be a shame to leave your home, travel a long distance, and face all kinds of risks and inconveniences all because of false opinion.

Is there any way to avoid having false opinions? The Stoics certainly thought so. In fact, they thought it was surprisingly simple. Just don't add anything to the basic facts, and you will avoid making most kinds of false judgments.

Not Adding Anything

The Stoic approach to critical thinking is highly pragmatic. It isn't based on abstract arguments but on the basic facts of everyday life. In one passage from his Discourses, Epictetus provides a simple key for applying Stoic thinking to anything that happens: "We ought to exercise ourselves daily against appearances for these appearances also propose questions to us. What do you think of it? It is a thing beyond the power of the will; it is not evil."

Every difficulty we face is an opportunity to practice, from a minor source of stress like a traffic jam to a major life event like a divorce. Epictetus even lists extreme misfortunes like being condemned to death and denies that they can be evil because they are not within the control of the will. This example is easier to understand if you think of a soldier. Soldiers swear to serve their country, and that sometimes means that they must die in battle. If dying were evil, it would always be good for soldiers to flee. By choosing to stand and fight against overwhelming odds, the soldier prioritizes duty and treats death as unimportant.

To face death with courage and dignity is good, but to die is indifferent. By adding a judgment of "good" or "bad" to a simple fact, you tie your happiness to something you cannot control. By not adding anything to the basic facts, you can turn everything that happens in life into something good.

You didn't get the promotion. What does that mean? That you didn't get the promotion and only that. You lost thousands of dollars. What does that mean? That you lost thousands of dollars and only that. Someone cut you off in traffic or said something bad to you, tried to trick you, or even stole from you. What do any of these things mean? They're all just facts, and any judgment we make about them is added afterward. To think like a Stoic, all you have to do is to avoid adding anything else to the bare facts.

Chapter 4: Self-Discipline and Resilience

"Be tolerant of others and strict with yourself."

- Marcus Aurelius

By this point in the book, you probably think that Stoicism sounds pretty hard to apply in practice. You're not alone. The ancient Stoics recognized certain people as Sages for their ability to apply Stoicism consistently in their daily lives. Epictetus himself denied being a

Sage because he could never quite get rid of anxiety about his health. His students must have been surprised by this statement because they asked him to name a real Sage. Perhaps sarcastically, he answered, "Hercules."

Any Stoic other than a Sage is called a *prokoptôn,* a "person making progress." When one of his students asked him the difference between a *prokoptôn* and a regular person, Epictetus said it was the same as the difference between drowning in 15 feet of water rather than 150 feet.

As you can see, Epictetus really didn't want his students to think of themselves as being close to Sagehood or as being wiser or more philosophical than other people. Stoicism is a process, and the most any of us can realistically hope is to make some progress toward the goal.

That doesn't mean Stoicism can't help you right now—far from it. If Epictetus himself was not a Sage, then you don't need to be a Sage either to benefit from Stoicism. The calm happiness and resilience of Stoic practice is available to everyone but only through rigorous self-discipline.

As Epictetus says, you would never think of competing in the Olympic Games without the necessary training that involves a lot of toughness and self-discipline. To take up philosophy is not so different and comes with its training methods.

In the practice of Stoicism, the training involves three specific disciplines.

The Three Disciplines of Stoicism

The Discipline of Desire: this means to restrict your desire to things that are under your own control. Whenever you find yourself desiring something that is not under your control—money, power, love, or admiration—transfer that feeling of desire to things that are under your own control. The desire for money can be changed into a determination to do a great job at work. The desire for power can be changed into a desire for justice, no matter who is in power. The desire for love can be changed into the desire to be a more loving person. The desire for the admiration of others can be changed into the desire to live an admirable life. In every case, you can take your yearning for something you can't control, and use it to fuel your determination to improve as a person and as a Stoic. Over time, you can teach yourself to stop desiring anything that isn't under your control.

The Discipline of Action: Stoicism distinguishes between actions that are "perfect" and actions that are merely "appropriate." Both types of action are correct, but the perfect action is done for the right reasons while the merely appropriate action is not. For example, if you don't cheat on your spouse because you don't want to get caught, your action is merely appropriate. If you don't cheat because you know it's wrong, your action is perfect. If you give money to charity so people will praise you, your action is merely appropriate. If you give money to charity for no other reason than to help other people, your action is perfect. The Sage's actions are always perfect, but the person making progress won't always be perfect. The discipline of action means to act appropriately, even when you aren't ready to take perfect actions. This is essentially a "fake it till you make it" approach. You might not be able to do the right thing with the right mentality, but you can, at least, make sure to do the right thing always. Don't think of this as hypocrisy but as practical training. Over time, the habit of doing the right thing should start to become second nature to you. More and more often, you will find yourself able to do the right thing for the right reason.

The Discipline of Assent: The discipline of assent is the Stoic practice of questioning first impressions, as in the examples given in the "Critical Thinking" chapter. By refusing to jump to conclusions about the things you experience, you can gain the distance you need to avoid being overwhelmed. Remember that Stoicism distinguishes between instinctive reactions and false judgments. There is an ancient story about a Stoic philosopher whose ship was caught in a deadly storm. When a huge wave smashed into the ship, the philosopher yelled as if he was scared. Questioned about his behavior after the incident, the Stoic said that his yell was due to an "impression" but that he had not "assented" to it. Whether he was telling the truth or not (and we'll never know!), the distinction is valid for any Stoic. You can't help having instinctive reactions, but whether you assent to them is up to you. Whenever you experience an emotional reaction, whether positive or negative, you should mentally pull back and ask yourself whether this involves something under your control or not. If it does not, be ready to say, "this is nothing to me."

The Three Disciplines can be summarized in a single sentence: restrict your desire to things you control, make sure your actions are always appropriate, and never assent too hastily to any impression.

Twelve Principles of Self-Discipline

The twelve principles discussed in this chapter are all derived from the *Enchiridion* or "Handbook" of Epictetus, one of the most accessible and useful works of ancient Stoicism. If you can remember and practice these twelve principles, you'll be well on your way to developing the self-disciplined and resilient mentality of the Stoic.

1: Control Desire
2: Keep Your Thoughts on the Ship
3: Remember That Nothing is Free
4: Let Them Laugh
5: Don't Reach for Things
6: Play Your Part

7: Avoid Envy

8: Don't Get Carried Away

9: Don't Show Off

10: Watch Yourself

11: Never Criticize Others

12: Accept Every Criticism

Control Desire

As Epictetus tells us, the feeling of desire includes the anticipation or "promise" of getting what you want. All too often, it's a false promise. If you desire something and you don't get what you desire, you'll feel disappointed. If you never want to feel disappointed, avoid desiring anything you can't be sure of getting. As Marcus Aurelius says, you can have an undefeated record in the battles of life if you never enter a battle that you aren't sure of winning. So, how can you avoid desiring things you can't be sure you'll get? The answer is through self-control and self-discipline.

Early on in your Stoic practice, Epictetus says you should "totally suppress" desire. Why does he make such an extreme statement? Desiring anything that is not under your control would only disappoint you and lead you away from Stoic practice while desiring anything under your control would be pointless until you develop more control in the first place. Desiring wisdom when you aren't capable of wisdom yet would have the same results as desiring anything else unobtainable.

Instead of desire, Epictetus says you should restrict yourself to pursuing the right things and avoiding the wrong things rationally. Even then, a beginner should pursue the right things calmly and gently, avoiding any violent emotions. Calm, unhurried patience is the basic mindset of Stoic practice.

Keep Your Thoughts on the Boat

How can you pursue anything without desiring it? Imagine you're a passenger on a ferry boat, visiting an island. When the boat docks, everyone gets off and looks around. When it's time for the last boat to leave the island and return to the mainland, a horn will sound. All the passengers know they need to listen for the horn, or they risk being left on the island until the next day.

In that situation, you might wander along the beach, looking at seashells or pretty rocks. You might climb a dune to get a look at the view. You might buy an ice cream cone or a souvenir at a little shop. The one thing you wouldn't do is ignore the horn because you wouldn't want to be stranded on the island.

As a practicing Stoic, it isn't necessary to live a life of grim privation. If anything seems fun or pleasant, you can pursue it within reason, as long as you remember what's important and avoid mistaking something trivial for something significant. Pretty seashells are nice, but they aren't important compared to listening for the horn. It's safe to look around and enjoy whatever you find, as long as you remember to keep your mind on the boat.

Remember That Nothing is Free

Nothing in life is ever free, and happiness is no exception. The price of happiness is Stoic discipline, and you pay the price whenever you react to a problem in a Stoic way. Rather than thinking about how much serenity costs, remind yourself of how valuable it truly is.

If a child knocks over an antique vase and smashes it, tell yourself, "that's the price of happiness." If an employee doesn't do something you asked them to do, tell yourself, "that's the price of serenity." If a neighbor comes over and yells at you about something trivial, tell yourself, "that's the price of tranquility."

Nothing is free, and the price of happiness is to control your reactions to the things that happen in life. Epictetus tells us to completely avoid "if-then" thoughts, such as, "if I don't get mad at my kids for breaking this vase, they won't be careful in the future," or, "if I don't come down hard on my employees, my business will fail."

Your children will learn a lot more by seeing how you handle stress than they will from any lecture you can give, but even if they don't, it's still better to have careless kids than to let it stress you out. Your employees will listen to a calm and self-controlled boss more willingly than an angry and abusive one, but even if they don't, it's better for your business to fail than for you to be unhappy.

Let Them Laugh

If you start to make progress in the Stoic way of life, other people will laugh at you. Let them laugh. Expect other people to see you as foolish or stupid. They'll say you're bad at business because you never get anxious about your business dealings. They'll say you're bad at dating because you never worry about who should call who first or how your partner might interpret something you said. They'll say you're bad at standing up for yourself because you don't get mad when people say or do insulting things.

Let them think of you as foolish because it doesn't matter. They're not going to understand your Stoic way of looking at things, and to act in a way they'd understand would mean giving up your Stoic practice.

If people aren't laughing at you for some reason, doubt yourself. Your calm and unruffled attitude could turn out to be an asset in business. Your unworried and natural demeanor might help you in dating. Your self-disciplined response to insults might earn the respect of those who previously looked down on you. These things aren't bad on their own, but they're still dangerous.

You can't pursue external things and internal things at the same time, so if you start to have a lot of success with external things, it's especially important not to attach your thoughts to them. If other people start to see you as someone important, wise, or admirable, tell yourself you are none of those things. It's safer for your Stoicism if they consider you a fool.

Don't Reach for Things

Imagine you're at a pleasant dinner party, with many fun things to eat and drink. If you see one of your favorites, would you reach across the table for it or just wait until it gets passed to you? Would you pile your plate high with everything you see or take a reasonable share so other people can enjoy it, too? If the host ran out of one of the items on the table before you got to taste it, would you complain bitterly or shrug and say, "maybe next time"?

The things people pursue in life are like food and drink at a dinner party. Don't reach out for them; just wait for them patiently, and enjoy them only in moderation. If they never come to you, don't worry about it, and just enjoy one of the other items. As

Epictetus says, "Do this with regard to children, to a wife, to public posts, to riches, and you will eventually be a worthy partner of the feasts of the gods."

Play Your Part

A person's life is like a play or a movie, but we don't get to write the story or pick our parts. Some movies are short, and some are longer. Some actors are admired for their beauty or talent while others have minor roles, and still, others are in the background. Some roles are tragic, some heroic, and some comedic. Whatever your part is, the most important point for an actor is to play the role naturally. Even if an actor only has a single line, he'll try to say that line as well as he can.

It's not in our power to pick our parts, but it is in our power to perform them well. As Marcus Aurelius says, your only other option is to make the audience laugh at you!

Avoid Envy

When a friend or a coworker gets something you don't, avoid envy and jealousy. If what they have is good, be happy for their sake. If it isn't good, there's nothing to be jealous of in the first place.

Everything has a price, and you can't expect to get the thing without paying the price for it. Does your boss seem to like your coworker better because of her shameless flattery? The flattery was the price of the boss's favor, and your coworker paid it. Your coworker now has what she paid for, but you still have your self-respect. Is a friend more successful at dating around? The price of that kind of success is to go out and flirt, to risk rejection repeatedly, and to pursue people actively. Your friend now has what he paid for, but you still have your self-control and dignity.

The things most people consider desirable have a high price tag for a Stoic because they would force him to act or think in a non-Stoic way. If you've set your sights on real happiness, you won't be willing to waste your time and energy on lesser things. Never envy anyone who is on a different path from you. If they believe those external things are more important, let them pay the price and enjoy what they've bought.

Don't Get Carried Away

Whenever you have the opportunity to enjoy something pleasurable, take care not to get carried away by it. Pause for a moment and think before you decide to indulge, comparing the short-term pleasure with the long-term consequences.

For example, you might have a few extra dollars to buy a pint of super premium ice cream. That's a tempting option, but if you sit down and eat a whole pint of ice cream by yourself, you'll probably feel sick and regret the extra calories.

After a stressful day, you might be tempted to go out to the bar and do some shots. The alcohol might make you feel better for a couple of hours, but you'll feel much worse in the morning, and you'll regret the decision.

While Stoics are not forbidden from doing pleasant things, even the most innocent pleasures should be questioned in this way. It can be useful for training purposes to exercise your self-control and refuse to indulge. In this situation, Epictetus tells us to compare the immediate pleasure of indulging with the much deeper joy of gaining more self-discipline and making progress in your practice of Stoicism.

Don't Show Off

If you stop indulging in things like alcohol and gourmet ice cream as often as others, people are likely to notice. Whatever you do, don't try to show off your newfound Stoicism. Don't lecture people about philosophy or act pretentious, showing off your knowledge of obscure and complicated books. Don't try to get people to notice how Stoic you are or to think of you as unusually tough or self-disciplined or philosophical.

The opinions of others are not under our control, and as such, they can neither be good nor bad. Cultivating a reputation as a Stoic would be the opposite of Stoicism, as a true Stoic wouldn't give any importance to external things like impressing other people.

If you keep your Stoicism low-key, you won't set yourself to fall when you make mistakes. As a person making progress rather than a Stoic Sage, you will make mistakes and make them often. It's better for people not to know you're a Stoic than to bring Stoicism into discredit and discourage others from giving it a try. If you waste your energy on trying to impress others with your Stoicism, you'll find it especially hard to put up with their mockery when you fall short.

Watch Yourself

Epictetus says to watch yourself as if you were an enemy waiting in ambush–and most people are, in fact, their own worst enemies. Knowing your tendency to chase after external things and to give value to things that have no real value, you always have to suspect your motivations. Whenever you want to do anything, ask yourself why you want to do it. Is this a rational choice or merely a pathos?

The more progress you make in Stoicism, the more people will start to notice something different about you. They may start to see you as someone with unusual self-control and calmness. They may even describe you as wise. If you listen to any of these voices, you'll lose everything you've gained so far. You should never let anyone describe you as someone important or as someone who knows everything. If anyone praises you, you should laugh at them—but not to their face, of course.

How can you tell when you're making progress? According to the Stoics, the beginner blames others, the person making progress blames himself, but the Sage blames no one.

Never Criticize Others

One of the foundational disciplines of Stoicism is to avoid criticizing other people for anything at all. A Stoic never blames or accuses anyone of doing something the wrong way. Without knowing the principles that motivate their actions, you cannot even be sure whether they're doing wrong. Rather than saying, "he drinks too much," you should say, "he drinks." Rather than saying, "she wastes her money," you should only say, "she spends her money." Restrict your comments to the facts, without attaching any blame or judgment.

The person you blame and judge could be a Sage in disguise, acting from perfect principles for reasons you don't understand. If you avoid judging and criticizing completely, you'll never have to regret making an unfair judgment of another person's actions.

Accept Every Criticism

Although you should never blame or criticize, you should always be ready to accept criticism from others without complaint or hurt feelings. As with other opinions, the judgments of other people are beyond your control and are therefore indifferent. If someone says something bad about you, the best response is to say something like this: "he must not know much about all my faults, or he would never have mentioned such a minor one."

Immune to criticism and to praise, the Stoic is completely free from the opinions of others. No one can make Stoics feel bad about themselves, and nothing can give them a swollen ego. Their focus is inward, pursuing the only thing that really matters—inner peace.

Chapter 5: Managing the Emotions

"We suffer more often in imagination than in reality."

\- Seneca

Stoic discipline is good for training, but the real test of this philosophy is how you react when things go wrong. Hardship happens to everyone, including Stoics. You will experience pain and illness. You will experience loneliness. People you love will someday die. What will you do when that happens?

The Stoics claimed that they could be happy under any circumstances. Perhaps a Sage could do that, but the philosophy should at least give you the tools to handle emotional turmoil with courage and dignity. If a negative emotion overwhelms you, remember the advice of Marcus Aurelius: you may not be able to act appropriately in every single moment, but if you do lose the way, you can always come back to it. Don't be disappointed if you slip up now and then, as long as you can see that you are steadily making progress. It's enough if most of your actions are in accord with reason. The rest will come with time.

Never be ashamed to ask for help if you need it: when a soldier stumbles on the battlefield, a nearby comrade will help him up. The only thing that matters is to keep moving forward, to keep making progress, and to keep improving.

With thoughts like these, the Stoic emperor overcame his own troubles and returned to his duties, winning one campaign after another along the Roman frontiers. Challenging emotions will come and go, but life continues. This selection of meditations from Seneca, Epictetus, and Marcus Aurelius should help you do the same.

Anxiety

The old saying "don't borrow trouble" seems like an echo of this thought from Seneca, the tutor and advisor to Emperor Nero: "He suffers more than necessary, who suffers before it is necessary."

Working for Nero would have made almost anyone anxious. The emperor was paranoid and had no real loyalty to anyone other than himself. Seneca did everything he could to reign in the emperor's worst impulses, but he did not succeed. In the end, Nero decided that Seneca had betrayed him and ordered the philosopher to commit suicide.

Seneca probably knew this was a possibility long before it happened, but his letters show no trace of anxiety. In all his *Epistles*, Seneca displays a calm and cheerful attitude. When Seneca tells us that we suffer more in imagination than in reality, he doesn't mean that our suffering is unreal somehow. He means that we add to our own suffering by anticipating it so anxiously.

Imagining all the frightening things that might happen will only add to our suffering. More often than not, the things we imagine don't end up happening anyway. Even if they do, worrying about them ahead of time won't help us deal with them. We do have the tools we need to meet them courageously, as long as we remember the lessons of Stoicism.

Accidents

Epictetus refers to the random incidents of life as "accidents" and reminds us that we always have some faculty that will allow us to meet any accident without harm to ourselves. The key to handling any accident is to apply the right tool for that particular accident.

For example, if you're married and you happen to meet an attractive person on a business trip, you can apply the faculty of self-restraint. If you have to spend time with a talkative and unpleasant person, you can apply patience. If you get hurt somehow and are in pain, you can apply fortitude.

The accidents Epictetus describes here are all fairly minor, but the same principle applies to much more challenging "accidents." Whatever happens, you can apply some tool to deal with it effectively. Through the rest of this chapter, think of every example given as a tool you can use, giving you the strength to face some hardship.

If you can do this, you should find it easier to deal with emotional turmoil when it arises. With enough practice, you can transform the accidents of life into new opportunities to make progress in Stoicism.

Welcome Trouble

In one of his letters, Seneca mentions that he is sick. Everyone in his house is sick. His income is declining, and his house is starting to get worn down. Instead of getting upset, he comments that such things are simply inevitable. Trouble happens to us all, and the longer you live, the more trouble you see. Getting sick or having a run-down house is nothing unusual for an older man, so he refuses to complain about such ordinary problems. Not only is Seneca content with all this, he actively welcomes it as an opportunity to practice his Stoicism.

If no trouble happened to us, we would never have the chance to test ourselves against adversity. We would never be sure of our inner strength, and any happiness we seemed to have would be insubstantial and unreliable. We could never be sure of what would happen if everything suddenly went badly wrong. Perhaps, we would fall apart as soon as we faced a serious test. In another letter, Seneca compares a life without trouble to a sea without wind: everything seems calm, but the boat isn't getting anywhere.

As a practicing Stoic, anything difficult that happens to you is like a chance to do battle, to prove yourself equal to the challenge. Like a sailor in a storm or a soldier on a campaign, you have the opportunity for heroism.

Check Your Principles

If death was as frightful as most people believe, why didn't it seem frightful to Socrates? With this simple question, Epictetus takes us back to the roots of

Stoicism in the courageous last hours of the great philosopher.

Death seems terrible to most people because they believe it to be terrible. Death didn't seem terrible to Socrates because he didn't believe it to be terrible. His principles told him not to flee from Athens, so he faced his death with unshakeable courage.

In all of life's great troubles, it is not the actual hardship that makes us sad, scared, or angry. It's always our own beliefs about what happened, our "principles" as Epictetus calls them.

Whenever anything disturbs or grieves you, don't blame the thing itself. Blame your beliefs about the thing. Check your principles on the topic in question, and correct them if there's anything wrong with them.

Is the thing that troubles you an internal matter, something you can fix through your own will? If it is, then fix it. Is it an external matter, something not under the control of your own will? If this is the case, then disregard it.

Hindrances

Epictetus refers to troubles and hardships as "hindrances," things that stand in the way. But what do they hinder?

If you think of them as hindrances to yourself, then you will be hindered. If you think of them as hindrances to something other than yourself, you will not be hindered. Stoicism encourages you to identify yourself with the ruling faculty, the ability to make rational choices, rather than with the body. The ruling faculty is under your control, but the body is not.

Is illness a hindrance to the body, or the ruling faculty? Most illnesses do not hinder the ability to make rational choices. Whenever you're ill, tell yourself, "this illness hinders my body, but it doesn't hinder my ruling faculty." If it doesn't hinder your ruling faculty, it doesn't hinder you.

Imagine you're injured and you can no longer use your leg. Does this hinder the leg or the ruling faculty? It obviously cannot hinder your ability to choose, so it only hinders your leg and not yourself.

You can do this with any physical problem that causes you difficulty in your daily life. Yes, the hindrance may put limitations on your movements. As long as it doesn't affect your ability to choose, you can remain free of any mental turmoil.

Insult

People get so agitated by insults and disrespectful behavior that they never stop to consider whether such things can injure them in the first place. Rising to every trivial provocation, they only end up making the situation worse. Damaged relationships and unnecessary drama are the inevitable consequence, but it can sometimes be worse than that. Much of the random violence in our society is driven by one simple error in judgment: the idea that an insult or act of disrespect can harm us. If a person insults you or does something you consider disrespectful, how will you react? Will you insult them back? Will you hit them?

Doing either of these things in response to an insult can have tragic consequences. When you decide to escalate a conflict, the other person can easily do the same. Road rage incidents and random arguments get out of control, and a minor incident becomes a tragedy. People go to prison every day because of their ideas about insults. People die.

Even in much less dramatic circumstances, responding emotionally to an insult can cause bigger problems. An argument with a friend or romantic partner can get out of hand as both people say hurtful things to each other, permanently damaging the relationship.

When you feel insulted, remember that you cannot be harmed by the insult itself, but you can be harmed by your ideas about it. Whatever discomfort or emotional distress you feel, it comes from your ideas about insults. If you can change those ideas, no insult will ever touch you.

Criticism

Harsh criticism can be hard to deal with, especially when it is not intended as an insult but as an honest critique or piece of advice. Imagine you're meeting an old friend for coffee, and your friend suddenly launches into a sweeping indictment of all your recent life decisions. Most people would probably feel upset and hurt to be judged like that. Perhaps the critique is a fair one, and perhaps it isn't. Perhaps your friend doesn't understand what happened or is making some unfair assumptions about your role in the situation.

Two plus two equals four, regardless of what anybody thinks. If a person is insisting that two plus two doesn't equal four, that person is harmed by his own ignorance, but the proposition isn't hurt at all. It just goes on being true.

If your friend was wrong about some choice you made, the truth cannot be changed or harmed by the misunderstanding. Whenever anyone harshly criticizes you, remind yourself that they were acting as they thought best based on their own understanding of the situation. They can't see the world through your eyes, and you can't see it through theirs.

Mistreatment

Some situations go beyond mere insult or criticism and into active mistreatment. You aren't obligated to let anyone mistreat you, and Stoicism should not be used as a reason to let yourself be abused. However, there are some situations where we may not feel it appropriate to let go of a certain relationship even though the other person is being extremely difficult to deal with. For example, if you're caring for an elderly parent who has dementia, they may say and do many hurtful things without even realizing it. A teenaged child might steal from your wallet or act out in other harmful ways. In these situations, Marcus Aurelius suggests a simple mental trick.

Imagine a heavy object with two handles—one large enough to pick it up with and one too small for that purpose. If you had to pick up that object, you wouldn't try to pick it up with the small handle, only with the large handle. The small handle is the feeling of being mistreated. The large handle is the relationship itself.

You can't deal with a difficult parent by thinking about how difficult they are but by reminding yourself that this person is your mother or father. You can't deal with a problem child by thinking about what a problem they are but by reminding yourself that this person is your child. Always use the larger handle.

Misfortune

If you feel unhappy because of something that happened to you, Marcus Aurelius suggests a series of questions.

Does this thing prevent you from being just? Does it prevent you from being generous? Does it prevent you from being temperate that allows you to respond to your problem in a calm and self-controlled way? Does it prevent you from being prudent? Does it force you to accept any false opinions or make any poor judgments? Does it take away your mental freedom?

If you can answer "no" to all these questions, then whatever happened has not truly harmed you. Someone else might have broken under the same pressure you just faced, but you didn't break. You're still here. Even if you didn't succeed in being completely Stoic, you haven't been thrown too far off course. Instead of being unhappy at your apparent misfortune, remind yourself to be happy that you have borne it well.

Contagious Emotions

Emotions can be contagious, especially negative emotions. You can become anxious by spending time with an anxious person or sad by spending time with a sad person—but only if you adopt their view of the matter.

To guard against this, Epictetus warns us not to get caught up in the intense emotions the people around us may be experiencing. If you see someone crying, by all means, try to help them somehow, but don't start crying along with them.

Instead, remind yourself that this person is crying because of the beliefs they hold and not because of whatever happened.

Ambition

If you're an ambitious person with big dreams and goals, it can be hard to watch other people earn the honors, promotions, or awards you've always dreamed of having. It's easy to start feeling envious or wonder why you haven't received the same kind of recognition. You may even start to feel depressed and self-critical, seeing yourself as a failure compared to others.

Ambition is a potent force, and there's nothing wrong with dreaming big. A Stoic practicing to become a Sage is an ambitious person, but she focuses her ambition on her actions and her own will. Rather than asking you not to dream big, Stoicism asks you dream even bigger. Don't set your sights on anything as limited and temporary as the recognition of others. Set your sights on becoming free, and don't be satisfied with anything less.

As Epictetus reminds us, there is only one battle where your success is under your control: the battle of the will. If you focus all your ambition on that battle, you can be sure of winning.

Difficult People

When you have to deal with an unreasonable person, Marcus Aurelius says that you should think of them as a training partner at a wrestling or boxing gym. Some training partners are unusually rough, and you might get extra bruises when you train with them. It's nothing personal. If anything, the need to protect yourself will keep you on your toes, and the training will be more valuable than usual.

If you think of a difficult coworker or family member as an especially rough training partner, you should find it easier not to lose your patience with them. You may even be grateful for the valuable training.

Illness

In one of his letters to Seneca, Lucilius challenges the Stoic teachings on illness and other hardships. According to the Stoics, a person can be happy under any circumstances—even when suffering the pain and discomfort of a serious illness. No one ever prays for illness or suffering. Doesn't that prove that such things are actually bad and not merely "indifferent"?

Seneca disagrees, pointing out that the happiness of the Stoic does not come from hardship but from the courage with which he is able to meet it:

"Nor am I so mad as to crave illness; but if I must suffer an illness, I shall desire that I may do nothing which shows lack of restraint... The conclusion is, not that hardships are desirable, but that virtue is desirable, which enables us patiently to endure hardships."

- Seneca

Severe illness can cause intense suffering, and no one would ever want to go through that experience. Even so, a Stoic can meet the challenge of illness with courage and fortitude, and that's where his happiness comes from.

Loss

The things we have in life are basically borrowed, and we never know when we'll have to give them back. That's true of everything from a childhood toy to the people you love the most. Sooner or later, you'll have to return all these things. Rather than thinking of a loss as something precious that has been taken away from you, think of it as a thing you borrowed and are now giving back. When you suffer some loss, whether large or small, you can apply this meditation to help you deal with it.

Instead of thinking, "I've lost my favorite book," tell yourself, "I've given it back."

Instead of thinking, "I've lost my job," tell yourself, "I've given it back."

Instead of thinking, "my pet has died," tell yourself, "I've given her back."

Epictetus suggests using this technique even with the most challenging of life's events such as divorce or a death in the family. As hard as it might be to apply this idea in such difficult circumstances, it's always healthy to remember that we don't own other people. We might feel like we've "lost" them, but the truth is we own only ourselves and our ability to make choices.

Grief

Seneca also addresses grief, perhaps with a little more empathy than the stern Epictetus. In one of his letters to Lucilius, Seneca seeks to comfort his student on the death of a close friend. Rather than asking him not to grieve at all, he asks him only to keep his grief within the limits of reason.

"Let not the eyes be dry when we have lost a friend, nor let them overflow. We may weep, but we must not wail."

- Seneca

Seneca does acknowledge the Stoic doctrine that the Sage could meet even the death of a close friend with total equanimity, but he is not so harsh as to insist that Lucilius live up to that demanding standard. He only tells him not to grieve too long or with any kind of melodramatic display.

Death comes to everyone, and almost all of us will lose friends and other loved ones at some point. To make sure we aren't surprised by grief, Seneca encourages Lucilius to keep the mortality of all his friends in the back of his mind. That way, when someone dies, we won't be so shocked that we lose our sense of balance.

Depression

> *"Sometimes, even to live is an act of courage."*
>
> *- Seneca*

While Stoicism can help with many of the problems that make people unhappy, clinical depression is not just a matter of feeling unhappy. If you suffer from depression, you may not have it in your power to reverse those feelings just by applying Stoicism.

On the other hand, you do have it in your power to handle depression the way a Stoic would. If you can't help being depressed, then it isn't under your control. What's under your control is how you respond to it. As with any other illness, it is possible to face your depression with Stoic courage.

Death

Most of us suffer from the fear of death to a greater or lesser degree. Marcus Aurelius was no exception. On campaign far away from home, he must have known that he could die in battle or from a disease, especially the disastrous Antonine Plague that killed five million Romans during his reign.

Many of the passages in the *Meditations* address the fear of death, implying that this was something the emperor struggled with frequently. In one passage, he reminds himself that the past and future are both illusions of the mind. The only thing that ever really exists is the present moment, and the only thing any of us can ever lose in death is the single moment in which we die.

The emperor's insight may or may not be helpful for you, but to a Stoic, the fear of death is like any other fear. You can't control the fact that you'll die someday, so death cannot be good or bad. Adopting this viewpoint can remove much of the fear.

Chapter 6: Great Stoics and Admirers of Stoicism

"Bitter are the roots of study, but how sweet their fruit."

- Cato

The Stoic way of life has inspired many people over the past 2300 years, including some of the most influential leaders in politics, sports, business, and the arts. Some of them practiced Stoicism as their daily philosophy, while others drew comfort and inspiration from the Stoic classics. From the committed Stoics to the merely curious, here are some of the greatest leaders and innovators who have applied the wisdom of Stoicism in their lives and careers.

Political Leaders

Considering that Stoicism is such a practical philosophy, it's not surprising that some of the greatest Stoics were political and military leaders rather than professional philosophers. In ancient times, the most influential and revered of these "practical Stoics" was probably Cato the Younger, a Roman statesman who fought to preserve the Republic and prevent the rise of Julius Caesar.

Cato was famous for his Stoic lifestyle, his uncompromising moral standards, and his physical courage. He dressed as a poor man, shoeless, and bareheaded in every weather. As a general of the Roman legions, he lived and worked as a common soldier. As a Senator, he refused bribes and scorned any attempt to influence his vote. When attacked by assassins during a Roman election, Cato refused to flee and made his way to the polls, still bleeding from his wounds.

Though some people mocked him at first for his inflexible rigidity, the consistency of Cato's character was deeply impressive. Over time, he gained so much moral authority that his fellow citizens saw him as the quintessential Roman and paid close attention to his opinion on any important issue. Unfortunately for Cato, he was unable to prevent the ambitious general and politician Julius Caesar from building popular support and assuming power.

When it became clear that Caesar would become the dictator of Rome—the development that eventually led to the end of the Republic and the birth of the Empire—Cato literally fell on his own sword in protest. Refusing all offers of help, he died as bravely as he had lived.

Cato was friends with another statesman named Cicero. Unlike Cato, Cicero was far from being a dogmatic Stoic. Despite being unwilling to commit completely to Stoicism, Cicero tried to live by Stoic principles in his career as a Roman politician. He was personally responsible for putting down a coup attempt through his decisive action in executing the leading conspirators. Just like Cato, Cicero was a defender of the Republic and an opponent of Caesar. Unlike Cato, Cicero outlived Caesar and went on to oppose his successor Mark Anthony.

Of course, the most famous Stoic political leader is probably Marcus Aurelius, who is remembered as the wisest and best of all the Roman emperors, as well as an important Stoic philosopher in his own right. To get some sense of what his life might have been like, watch the first scene of the movie *Gladiator*—the wise old emperor at the beginning of the movie is supposed to be him.

When Stoicism faded out of public awareness as the Roman Empire became Christian, leaders turned to other sources of inspiration for a time. The Renaissance brought Stoicism back into the public eye, and eventually, the Stoic classics became a standard part of the educational curriculum and influenced generations of leaders.

American president Theodore Roosevelt, in his long and grueling mission to explore the River of Doubt in the Amazon rain forest, brought only eight books in his luggage. One of those books was by Epictetus and another by Marcus Aurelius.

Chinese prime minister Wen Jiabao, in an interview with *Newsweek*, revealed that he had read the *Meditations* of Marcus Aurelius over a hundred times. Other leaders who have claimed to be inspired by the Stoics—whether or not they actually lived according to Stoic principles—include Thomas Jefferson, Bill Clinton, and Cory Booker.

Military Leaders

The Prussian ruler and military leader Frederick the Great took up the practice of Stoicism in a moment of despair after his armies were nearly wiped out in the Seven Years War of 1756-1763. Going on to eventual triumph and great renown as a general, Frederick was so grateful to Marcus Aurelius for his inspiration that he filled his summer home with statues of the philosopher-emperor and referred to Marcus Aurelius as his personal hero. Frederick the Great wasn't exactly a Stoic—his ambition for glory wasn't Stoic at all—but he was able to use Stoic principles to overcome disaster and go on to victory.

During the American Revolution, George Washington used his admiration for Cato the Younger to rally his dispirited troops at Valley Forge. Cato the Younger was a hugely popular figure among the American leaders, who saw him as a symbol of both the Stoic virtues and resistance to tyranny. Washington arranged for a play about Cato's life to be performed for the troops, inspiring them to endure the winter at Valley Forge with the same Stoic resolve Cato the Younger would have shown.

Washington wasn't the only leader of that period to be inspired by the Stoics. Toussaint Louverture, one of the leading figures in the Haitian War of Independence against Napoleon's France, was said to have been guided by his study of Epictetus. Incidentally, the Haitian Revolution is still the only successful slave rebellion in human history, so the writings of the slave Epictetus influenced the liberation of the Haitian slaves many centuries after the philosopher's death.

More recently, Vice Admiral James Stockdale used the teachings of Epictetus to help him endure his seven years of captivity at the "Hanoi Hilton" POW prison in North Vietnam. Stockdale's fortitude and courage in this situation are legendary. He not only held up under torture repeatedly but succeeded in inspiring his fellow prisoners to commit to unyielding resistance against their captors. Later in life, Stockdale could still recite any passage of Epictetus's "Handbook" from memory.

The writings of the Stoics remain popular with soldiers. According to Nancy Sherman, a Professor of Philosophy who wrote a book called *Stoic Warriors: The Ancient Philosophy Behind the Military Mind*, the works of Epictetus are especially popular with soldiers because of his straightforward and unpretentious style. Former Defense Secretary James Mattis carried a copy of the *Meditations* of Marcus Aurelius in his rucksack as a young soldier and credited it with helping him endure the hardships of combat. While serving as Defense Secretary, he described it as the one book every American should make a point of reading.

Entertainers

Although Stoicism offers the most to those who practice it wholeheartedly, the Stoic classics can provide support and emotional resilience to anyone who reads them. Several popular entertainers have expressed an interest in Stoicism or one of the Stoic thinkers. For example, Anna Kendrick—singer, actor, and author of *Scrappy Little Nobody*—turns to Marcus Aurelius for emotional comfort even though she doesn't consider herself a practicing Stoic. In a *New York Times* interview, Kendrick described the *Meditations* as a "soothing" book, even though she doesn't agree with everything Marcus Aurelius has to say.

You can get a lot of great advice for daily life just by keeping a copy of one of the Stoic classics by your bed and reading a short passage every night before you go to sleep. That's probably why Thomas Jefferson had one of Seneca's books on his nightstand when he died, but he's not the only one to keep the Stoics close at hand. Brie Larson of *Community* and *21 Jump Street* tweeted a screenshot of one of her favorite passages from Marcus Aurelius in 2017. The passage she chose was about philosophy as a guide for daily life, encouraging her fans and Twitter followers to find out more about the Stoics.

Similarly, English actor Tom Hiddleston tweeted a screenshot from Seneca's "On the Shortness of Life" in 2011, adding that the Stoic philosopher "knew a thing or two." In this passage, Seneca talks about how different people are driven by different things—greed, ambition, or simple restlessness—but few are capable of simply slowing down and enjoying their lives. According to Seneca, life only seems so short to us because we spend most of it distracted. Hiddleston has appeared in Marvel superhero movies such as *Thor* and *The Avengers* and was the star of the BBC miniseries *The Night Manager*.

Stoicism seems to be especially popular among hip hop performers. Lupe Fiasco mentioned Marcus Aurelius in the track "Lightwork," and encouraged fans to read *Meditations* first if they wanted to talk to him. Twista claimed to be "as sick as" Marcus Aurelius in his track "Get Me," and rap superstar LL Cool J is a fan of Neo-Stoic self-help guru Ryan Holiday.

Stoicism is also in vogue with at least a few major R&B performers, including Grammy-winning T-Pain, creator of the album *Stoicville: The Phoenix* and the mixtape *Stoic*. T-Pain has stated that he identifies with the Stoic's ability to endure pain without complaint. Dutch musician and artist Nick van Hofwegen, also known as Young & Sick, helped the Daily Stoic blog design a poster based on a quote from Marcus Aurelius.

These entertainers might not be deeply involved in the Stoic practice, but they have all drawn on Stoic ideas to one degree or another in dealing with the ups and downs of life in the public eye. By using their fame to promote the works of Seneca or Marcus Aurelius, they may influence at least some of their fans to give Stoicism a try.

Athletes

Stoicism has been surprisingly influential in the world of professional sports, largely due to a chance gift NFL executive Michael Lombardi received from his wife. When she gave him a copy of the *Meditations* of Marcus Aurelius for Christmas one year, the two-time Superbowl winner became so intrigued that he took a challenge to try to live like a Stoic for 30 days. Lombardi went on to take a course in Stoicism from writer and teacher Donald Robertson, author of *How to Think Like a Roman Emperor*.

Lombardi began to encourage other people in professional football to study the Stoics, especially the members of the New England Patriots. Rather than asking the players to read the original Stoic classics,

Lombardi encouraged them to read *The Obstacle is the Way* by Ryan Holiday, which updates and popularizes Stoicism as a "life-hack" or technique for modern people to improve their lives.

The book proved to be highly popular with Tom Brady and the other players, who used it to overcome the widespread public criticism of the team over the Deflategate controversy. When the Patriots beat the Seattle Seahawks to win the Superbowl, they were kind enough to recommend the book to their defeated rivals. Seattle Seahawks head coach Pete Carroll has since become known for his interest in Stoicism, as has Seahawks General Manager Schneider. Holiday's work is now popular throughout the NFL.

Interest in Stoicism is spreading to college football as well. University of Alabama coach Nick Saban relies on the advice of Marcus Aurelius, as well as on Ryan Holiday's modern interpretation.

In an interview with *Sports Illustrated* about his interest in Stoicism, Lombardi points out that great leaders in all areas of life are always looking for new ways to improve their leadership qualities. Studying the great leaders of the past is an obvious choice—the ideas that helped Marcus Aurelius in his wars with the enemies of Rome can certainly help the New England Patriots in their struggles with other teams. Lombardi didn't stop with Marcus Aurelius; in the same interview, he also mentions reading and enjoying Seneca.

Interest in Stoicism among professional athletes and coaches is not confined to football. Chicago Cubs manager Joe Maddon is a fan of Holiday's version of Stoicism, as is University of Texas basketball coach Shaka Smart. Chandra Crawford, a cross-country skier and Olympic gold medalist, is also known as a practicing Stoic.

Stoicism's appeal to athletes isn't hard to understand. Athletes have to engage in harsh training to achieve their goals, and all athletes experience both defeats and victories. A philosophy like Stoicism is ideally suited to the athlete's lifestyle, giving them the mental fortitude to handle both the rigors of training and the uncertainties of competition. Marcus Aurelius and Epictetus both use athletic metaphors in their works on Stoicism. Epictetus compares training in Stoic philosophy to training for the Olympics, and Marcus Aurelius suggests treating difficult people as unusually rough training partners. The connection between athletics and Stoicism may have been just as clear in ancient times as it is today.

Authors

Most writers are also voracious readers, and some of the most influential writers of all time have counted the works of the Stoics among their favorite books.

Ambrose Bierce, the author of the satirical classic *The Devil's Dictionary*, was fond of the *Enchiridion* of Epictetus. In a letter to a friend, he echoed a passage from that work by saying that the study of Stoicism would make him worthy of being a dinner guest of the gods themselves. Bierce is mostly remembered today for his witty and cynical definitions of common words, but he was also a journalist, poet, and author of powerful short stories about the Civil War.

John Steinbeck, the author of some of the greatest American novels ever written, has one of his characters read a passage from Marcus Aurelius in his 1952 novel *East of Eden*. Steinbeck described the *Meditations* as one of his two favorite books.

JK Rowling—perhaps the most famous writer of modern times for her Harry Potter series—has also described herself as a fan of Marcus Aurelius.

Of course, being a fan of a book is one thing, and incorporating its ideas into your own life is another. Author and philosopher Ralph Waldo Emerson was a fan of the Stoics, but he also incorporated some of their ideas when developing his own philosophy of Transcendentalism.

More recently, philosopher Nassim Nicholas Taleb has mentioned his love of Seneca in two of his works– *The Black Swan* (which deals with the often world-changing consequences of highly improbable events) and *Antifragile* (which explores societies and systems resilient enough to avoid sudden collapse).

Robert Greene (author of *The 48 Laws of Power*) and Neil Strauss (author of *The Game: Penetrating the Secret Society of Pickup Artists*) have also expressed enthusiasm for Stoicism, though it should be noted that neither pickup artists nor power-seekers can be described as Stoics.

Business Leaders

Stoicism began when Zeno of Citium took up philosophy to console himself after losing his fortune in a disastrous shipwreck. He later described this shipwreck as the most profitable voyage he had ever undertaken. Stoicism can help entrepreneurs and business leaders overcome adversity and achieve the heights of professional success. Paradoxically, it does so by teaching them to stop getting emotionally invested in concepts like defeat and victory and profit and loss.

In the words of Musonius Rufus, the Stoic teacher of Epictetus, "the person in training must seek to rise above, so as to stop seeking out pleasure and steering away from pain; to stop clinging to living and abhorring death; and in the case of property and money, to stop valuing receiving over giving."

By detaching from the endless pursuit of profit and competition with other companies, the Stoic business leader can see things as they truly are and act appropriately. Stoicism does not teach us to ignore our roles in society just because they are "indifferent" to genuine happiness.

A Stoic emperor cannot neglect his duties but must seek to govern wisely and well—as Marcus Aurelius did. A Stoic businessperson, without allowing himself to think of profit as good and loss as bad, must still conduct the affairs of his company with all the skill and strategic intelligence he can manage. As Epictetus says, we don't get to pick our roles in the play of life, but we still need to perform them with all our skill.

Several prominent business leaders have been inspired by Stoicism. Jack Dorsey, a co-founder of Twitter, is one of several well-known tech leaders who are admirers of Stoicism. Others include Foundry Group investor Brad Feld and GoDaddy CEO Blake Irving, as well as many lesser-known designers and engineers in Silicon Valley. In fact, Stoicism has become so popular among Silicon Valley tech workers that it inspired an article on the topic by *Quartz's* Olivia Goldhill.

Kevin Rose, a highly successful investor and entrepreneur, is a fan of the book *The Ego is the Enemy* by modern Stoic Ryan Holiday. Angel investor Tim Ferriss is so enthusiastic about Stoicism that he republished Seneca's *Epistles* under the title *The Tao of*

Seneca, and recorded excerpts from Seneca's letters on his own podcast.

Condé Nast CEO Jonathan Newhouse won't travel without copies of the Stoic classics on hand. David Heinemeier Hansson, the founder of project management company Basecamp, mentioned his admiration for the Stoics in an interview with Tim Ferriss.

Stoicism: Life-Hack or Way of Life?

As you can see, Stoicism has appealed to many people, including some who have had a tremendous influence. If George Washington had never been inspired by the example of Cato the Younger, who knows if the United States would even exist? If Frederick the Great had not turned to Stoicism after his early defeats, would he have ever gone on to win his greatest victories?

Although Stoicism has given courage and fortitude to some of the greatest leaders, writers, and even entertainers, there's a difference between using Stoicism as a "life hack" to make you more effective and practicing Stoicism as a way of life. Kai Whiting and Leonidas Konstantakos, writing for the "Partially Examined Life" blog, encourage readers interested in Stoicism to take their interest deeper. You can turn to Stoicism for comfort and inspiration when things don't go well, and you can use it to give you the fortitude to overcome a challenge and go on to victory. But, neither of these things can produce genuine and lasting happiness.

Epictetus once described students with "a little philosophy" as the most challenging of all, since they were harder to help than students with no experience. He also described the condition of a "person making progress" as being similar to drowning in shallow water—you're closer to safety, but you're not there yet.

If you don't completely agree with Stoicism, you can still apply the parts of it you do agree with to help you live a better and more fulfilling life. That's what Cicero did, despite going on record as a critic of some Stoic ideas. If Stoicism does strike you as a valid philosophy, you'll probably get a lot more out of it by practicing it seriously than by using it as a mere technique for getting ahead in life. As Whiting and Konstantakos point out in their article, the pursuit of success for its own sake binds you to something not under your control. According to Stoicism, this makes it impossible for you to be free or happy.

If you pursue Stoicism with a full commitment, you may also end up being a success in business or whatever field you decide to pursue. The clear-headed mentality of Stoicism can be a tremendous asset. If you pursue Stoicism half-heartedly, you may find yourself unsuccessful at both career and philosophy. As Epictetus says, it's not possible to put equal effort and intensity into two separate goals.

This is not to imply that you cannot have a career while pursuing Stoicism. The Stoics believed it was possible to practice philosophy within the everyday world of career and family, or they would never have split away from the Cynics over that issue. However, your best chance of achieving both happiness and success is to focus on happiness, letting success happen along the way. The Stoic approach to life and work is one of the most enduring guides to making that happen.

Chapter 7: Stoicism and Psychology

> "The philosophical origins of cognitive therapy can be traced back to the Stoic philosophers."
>
> - Aaron T. Beck

Everyone has not welcomed the renewed popularity of Stoicism. Stoicism is sometimes criticized as an outdated philosophy, a relic of ancient thinking with no place in the modern world. Some people say it's unrealistic, that we can't really control our emotions just by changing our belief system. Other people say we shouldn't even try and that Stoicism would keep us from ever experiencing love or joy. Does Stoicism increase good feelings as its practitioners claim, or does the rejection of the passions lead to a gray life with no emotional depth?

The great Stoics, like Epictetus, taught that our thoughts are the main source of our happiness and unhappiness in life. So, how well does Stoicism match up with what we know about the brain? If Stoic ideas have any validity, they should be confirmed by modern psychology and cognitive science.

There are many different therapies in the practice of psychology, including everything from traditional Freudian psychotherapy to acceptance and commitment therapy. One of the most effective and widely used treatments is known as Cognitive Behavioral Therapy or CBT.

CBT is used in the treatment of anxiety, mood disorders, eating disorders, depression, gambling addiction, substance abuse, and many other common problems. Studies have shown it to be one of the most effective and practical types of therapy, and it is considered the preferred treatment for a wide range of cognitive and behavioral issues. Studies have shown it to be just as effective as medication in some cases, making it the ideal option for people who want to address their problems without medication if possible.

Although CBT is a treatment method rather than a philosophy, the core ideas of this therapy are based on ancient Stoicism. Practicing Stoicism is not the same thing as receiving treatment in Cognitive Behavioral Therapy from a qualified professional, and receiving CBT treatment won't make you a philosopher. The two are distinct. Nevertheless, the tools CBT therapists use are based on the insights of Epictetus, Seneca, and Marcus Aurelius—a powerful argument for the validity of the Stoic worldview.

Cognitive Behavioral Therapy is a broad term, encompassing several different methods. Cognitive Emotional Behavioral Therapy, Structured Cognitive Behavioral Training, Moral Reconation Therapy, Stress Inoculation Training, Unified Protocol, Mindfulness-based Cognitive Behavioral Hypnotherapy, and Brief Cognitive Behavioral Therapy are all types of CBT.

All these therapies have slightly different theories and techniques, and some incorporate other influences along with Stoicism. For instance, Mindfulness-based Cognitive Behavioral Hypnotherapy incorporates some ideas from Buddhism. However, the basic insights and assumptions of CBT are shared by all the variations, and all of them share the same roots in ancient Stoicism.

Development of CBT

CBT can be traced back to an earlier method called Cognitive Therapy, which is now considered one of the subtypes of CBT. Cognitive Therapy was developed in the 1960s by a psychoanalyst named Aaron Beck, who felt that traditional psychotherapy was too focused on the unconscious to be practical for most patients.

Beck's reading of the Stoics had convinced him that psychological problems are often influenced by how people think and what they believe about the world. This matches several passages in the *Meditations* of Marcus Aurelius, where the emperor reminds himself that our beliefs and opinions are the prime cause of all our actions.

According to Beck, negative feelings and behaviors are often the direct consequence of negative beliefs and thoughts. He wanted to help patients recognize distorted thought patterns so that they could transform them over time into more positive and functional thought patterns. Beck believed that this would naturally lead to a decrease in dysfunctional behaviors, making Cognitive Therapy an effective treatment for substance abuse and other behavioral problems.

Cognitive Therapy is based on Beck's Cognitive Model, which divides human thought into three categories: automatic thoughts, intermediate beliefs, and core beliefs. Automatic thoughts are involuntary negative reactions based on the patient's underlying beliefs about the self, other people, or the future.

For example, a person suffering from an eating disorder might have a feeling of revulsion and self-hatred when looking in a mirror, imagining herself to be much heavier than she really is. Automatic thoughts derive from intermediate beliefs in an "if-then" pattern, for example, "if I lose enough weight, I'll finally be popular." Intermediate beliefs derive from core beliefs such as, "nobody likes me." By tracing the automatic thought all the way back to the core belief that ultimately inspired it, it becomes clear that this patient's eating disorder is based in a deep belief that she is unlikeable and that treating this belief is key to treating the behavior.

In Cognitive Therapy, the therapist helps the patient learn to recognize automatic thoughts, then identifies the intermediate and core beliefs driving automatic thoughts. By asking a series of questions (a method borrowed from Socrates), the therapist demonstrates the irrational nature of these beliefs. Finally, the therapist helps the patient understand that these beliefs and automatic thoughts are distorted and inaccurate.

This process mirrors the Stoic approach to cognition, in which automatic reactions or "impressions" are subjected to questioning and only "assented to" if they seem rational by Stoic standards. Essentially, the Cognitive Therapist teaches the patient to question his impressions and assent only to those who turn out to be rational after close examination. Epictetus would certainly approve.

Cognitive Behavioral Therapy takes the basic idea of Cognitive Therapy and adds additional techniques from Behaviorism, especially the use of desensitization and conditioning techniques to help patients overcome neuroses such as phobias. The Cognitive aspect of CBT is the aspect most heavily influenced by Stoic philosophy, but the Behaviorist aspect has proven to be very helpful for patients suffering from deep underlying fears and compulsions.

Thoughts, Emotions, and Actions

In the CBT model of how the mind works, thoughts influence emotions, and emotions influence actions or behaviors. Our actions confirm our thoughts about the world, and the cycle then repeats itself.

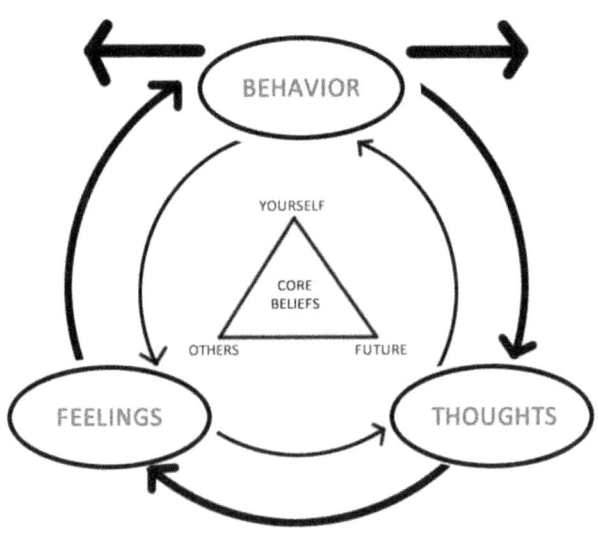

Attribution: Urstadt at English Wikipedia, licensed under the Creative Commons Attribution-Share Alike 3.0 Unported license.

For example, you might think that you can't relax and destress without some wine. This thought leads you to feel stressed out and tense until you do drink some wine, at which point, you feel a little bit more relaxed. The next time you have the same thought, you're more likely to act on it because your experience of drinking the wine confirmed the validity of the thought. Of course, drinking too much wine causes other problems over time, but it's hard to break out of the loop because the connection between thought, feeling, and action seems so convincing. Even if you suspect that drinking too much is ultimately causing you much more stress, it's hard for you to accept that it won't help you right now.

At a deeper level, CBT holds that our core beliefs drive our thoughts. As in Cognitive Therapy, core beliefs are divided into three categories: beliefs about the self, beliefs about other people, and beliefs about the world. For example, the thought that it is not possible to relax without wine might be driven by core beliefs that the world is a threatening and stressful place, that other people cannot or will not offer emotional support, and that you can't rely on anyone except yourself when you feel overwhelmed. Not knowing any other ways to relax effectively, you then convince yourself that drinking wine is the only realistic option.

This is only a simplified version of how CBT works, but the connection to Stoicism is easy to see. Epictetus would certainly agree that our core beliefs about the world inform our opinions about specific situations, generating negative emotions or *pathé*, such as fear, and finally leading us to make unhealthy decisions. Stoicism and Cognitive Behavioral Therapy share the same basic and practical assumption that our actions are driven mostly by what we believe about the world, and the most effective way to make positive changes in our life is to change what we believe. However, CBT does not focus on the central doctrine of Stoicism that all cognitive distortions ultimately come from the same source.

Cognitive Distortions

The main difference between the Stoic approach and the CBT approach is in the definition of what makes a thought "distorted" or unhelpful. In classical Stoicism, defining anything outside your own control as "good" or "bad" is a cognitive distortion. This is the basic error the Stoic wants to avoid. In CBT, there are four types of cognitive distortion: catastrophizing, overgeneralizing, minimizing positives, and maximizing negatives.

Catastrophizing is a type of if-then thinking in which the worst-case scenario is assumed to be true without any evidence. For example, "if I don't keep my house spotlessly clean, I'll catch a disease and die," or "if I don't get this report perfect, I'll be fired, and my career will be ruined."

Overgeneralizing is drawing a sweeping conclusion without enough evidence to support the conclusion. For example, if you go to a party, and no one talks to you, it would be an overgeneralization to assume that no one ever likes you or wants to talk to you. Your experience at a single party just isn't enough evidence for the generalization.

Minimizing positives is the habit of disregarding any evidence that things are going well for you. For instance, you might tell yourself that your new promotion doesn't matter because you'll just be overwhelmed with stress and mess things up.

Maximizing negatives is the habit of focusing too much on whatever is difficult or challenging in your life. For example, you might tell yourself you're all alone because you don't have a girlfriend, ignoring the fact that you have several close friends.

The four cognitive distortions of CBT do show some influence from Stoicism. Marcus Aurelius and Epictetus both warn us not to indulge in any "what if" thinking but to stick to the basic facts about the situation. It's not harmful to say, "my mother is sick," but it is harmful to say, "my mother is sick; what if she dies?" Avoiding "what if" thinking prevents catastrophizing.

Sticking to the facts is also a good defense against overgeneralizing. "I went to the party, and no one talked to me" is just a fact, with no value judgment attached to it. "I went to the party, and no one talked to me because no one ever wants to talk to me" is an overgeneralization. By just not adding anything to factual account, you can avoid this type of cognitive distortion.

The other two types of cognitive distortion are a bit more distant from Stoic thought because a Stoic would never admit that any external event could be positive or negative in the first place. Minimizing positives would just be "minimizing preferred *indifferents*," and maximizing negatives would just be "maximizing dispreferred *indifferents*." The Stoic way of thinking about life doesn't grant any true importance to either one.

That's the difference between Stoicism as a philosophy and CBT as a therapy. To practice Stoicism, you have to accept Stoic teachings about what really matters and what does not. Without accepting that virtue is the only good, it would be hard to practice Stoicism. To benefit from CBT, you don't have to accept any particular belief. You just have to be willing to question your existing beliefs with the therapist's help and guidance.

Cognitive Behavioral Therapy is a practical application of Stoic insights for people who don't necessarily know anything about Stoicism.

Stages of Cognitive Behavioral Therapy

Cognitive Behavioral Therapy begins with an assessment, in which the therapist attempts to determine which critical behaviors are having an effect on the client's life. Next, the therapist decides whether these behaviors are excessive or deficient—too much or too little for the real situation. The therapist finds out how often the behavior is happening, how long it usually lasts, and how intense it is. This becomes the baseline, and the goal of the therapy is then to increase or reduce the frequency of the behavior based on the circumstances.

For example, the behavior might be excessive handwashing, a typical compulsive symptom. The therapist would find out how often the client washes his hands and how much time he spends doing so. The goal of therapy would be to reduce the frequency and duration of the behavior, so it stops causing problems in the client's life.

The next phase in CBT is reconceptualization, where the client is encouraged to think about his problem differently. This phase is similar to the Stoic approach because it's based on changing the client's beliefs about the world.

This phase is followed by skill acquisition, where the patient practices specific exercises to help him modify the behavior. Once these skills are consolidated, the therapist helps the patient generalize what he has learned in therapy. By learning how to spot the four basic cognitive distortions, the patient is given the tools to become his own therapist in the future.

That doesn't mean it's all smooth sailing from this point forward. Patients typically need some follow-up sessions to make sure they haven't slipped back into old ways of thinking.

Stoicism in Positive Psychology

Of course, Cognitive Behavioral Therapy only supports Stoicism to a limited extent because the creators of CBT didn't incorporate every aspect of Stoicism into the practical therapies they were designing. The success of CBT suggests that Stoicism is right about a few key points, especially that our happiness or unhappiness is largely determined by our beliefs.

However, CBT's effectiveness cannot be interpreted as evidence for Stoicism's most important assertions. For that, psychologists would need to test Stoicism itself, not a therapy derived from Stoicism. The purpose of therapy is to correct a disorder, but the goal of philosophy like Stoicism is to achieve well-being and happiness. This is the domain of positive psychology, a movement to redirect psychology away from the exclusive study of psychological disorders and toward the study of human well-being. Some researchers in this field have decided to test whether Stoicism can live up to its claims and improve people's lives.

In 2013, Professor Christopher Gill of the University of Exeter conducted a research study on the benefits of Stoicism with Tim LeBon of the Modern Stoicism website. The goal of the study was to determine whether Stoic training would help participants experience more life satisfaction and more positive emotions.

Participants in the study were taught the basics of Stoic practice and assigned a set of daily exercises. Exercises included a morning meditation on Stoic principles, daily study of Stoic principles and techniques, a Stoic worksheet, and evening meditation on things done well and poorly during the day. All these exercises were based on specific passages in the Stoic classics.

Some of the participants were recruited from existing Stoic discussion groups, and others were recruited from the public at large. The study lasted for a single week, after which participants were asked a series of questions to determine what effect a one-week training course in Stoicism had on their daily lives.

At the end of the week, the amount of life satisfaction reported by participants had increased by 14%. The frequency/intensity of negative emotion was down by 11%, and the frequency/intensity of positive emotion was up by 9%. Feelings of optimism were up by 18%, and 56% of participants described themselves as having behaved more ethically than usual. These are significant improvements for a study that lasted for just a single week, providing strong scientific support for

Stoicism as a path toward increased well-being, happiness, and virtue.

The Stoic Attitudes and Behaviors Self-Rating Scale

In an attempt to further study the relationship between Stoicism and well-being, modern Stoic Donald Robertson has developed the Stoic Attitudes and Behaviors Self-Rating Scale or SABSS. This scale is a test anyone can take at home to determine how closely their own beliefs match Stoic attitudes.

The SABSS test consists of 20 statements about Stoic beliefs and attitudes, followed by 10 statements about Stoic behaviors and life strategies. There is also one question to determine whether participants consider themselves to be practicing Stoics. Depending on the individual, identifying as a Stoic may or may not go along with holding Stoic principles or using Stoic strategies.

Participants are asked to rate every statement on a scale of one to five, with five meaning "strongly agree" and one meaning "strongly disagree." This allows shades of agreement and disagreement with Stoic principles. For instance, you might give a five rating to the statement that the goal of life is happiness but a three to the statement that virtue is the only thing needed for happiness.

Study of the SABSS questionnaire has produced some interesting results. As Stoicism predicts, prioritizing pleasure over virtue seems to be correlated with low levels of happiness and well-being. Stoic beliefs and attitudes were correlated with higher levels of happiness. However, Stoic life strategies and behaviors turned out to be more important for well-being than Stoic beliefs.

The study is not yet enough to establish causality, but it seems to imply that living like a Stoic will do more for your overall well-being than simply thinking like a Stoic. Given a choice between Stoic habits and Stoic beliefs, you should focus on building good habits and let the beliefs take care of themselves. Cognitive Behavioral Therapy teaches us that thoughts, emotions, and actions are all part of a feedback loop. By taking Stoic types of action, you can change your thoughts, which will result in changing your feelings as well.

Stoic Habits

The SABSS study identified four specific Stoic habits as most important in promoting happiness and overall well-being.

The first was "mindfulness," defined as paying close attention to your actions and to the judgments you make in daily life. Rather than acting without thinking or making judgments without consideration, you should carefully weigh both your thoughts and acts.

The second was questioning your mental impressions before assenting to them. The ancient Stoics compared this practice to a sentry questioning anyone who approaches the guard-post. Don't let just any thought come in through the gate—be suspicious of your impressions.

The third was thinking of yourself as part of the social whole rather than an isolated individual. Marcus Aurelius talks about this constantly in his *Meditations*, reminding himself that "whatever does not harm the hive does not harm the bee."

The fourth was negative visualization, desensitizing yourself to potentially upsetting experiences by imagining them ahead of time. This practice could be the original inspiration behind the desensitization practices in Cognitive Behavioral Therapy. Of course, it's important not only to visualize whatever scares you but also to visualize yourself handling it in a Stoic way. It wouldn't do you any good to visualize breaking down or going into a tailspin of negative emotions!

These four practices on their own are an excellent introduction to the Stoic practice. Be mindful of your actions and judgments, be suspicious of your impressions, think of yourself as part of a social whole, and imagine the worst before it happens. With such a simple set of daily goals, anyone can get started practicing Stoicism right away.

In Stoic practice, right actions done for the wrong reason are merely appropriate, while right actions done for the right reason are referred to as "perfect." Appropriate behavior is the first step toward happiness, and perfect behavior is the culmination. The SABSS study suggests that appropriate behavior is enough to bring significant improvements in your life even if you aren't yet capable of perfect behavior.

In practical terms, this means that a "person making progress" can become significantly happier by practicing Stoicism and that greater well-being and freedom are not restricted to the Sage.

While many more studies will have to be done before we can say anything definitive about the effects of Stoic practice, there is certainly enough evidence to be optimistic. Rather than being an outdated and irrelevant philosophy from the distant past, Stoicism is beginning to receive support from the most up-to-date research in positive psychology.

Chapter 8: Everyday Stoicism

> *"Let sleep not come upon thy languid eyes Before each daily action thou hast scann'd; What's done amiss, what done, what left undone; From first to last examine all, and then Blame what is wrong in what is right rejoice."*
>
> *- Epictetus*

Now that you understand the basics of Stoicism and how Stoics go about dealing with daily problems and emotional turmoil, you might be wondering how to get started. The Stoic idea is surprisingly simple, but making progress as a Stoic is not so simple. As with any skill, Stoic thinking takes a lot of practice. These simple exercises are not absolutely required in the practice of Stoicism but are likely to be helpful in the early stages. Some of them might seem a little harsh and puritanical the first time you read them, but they are based on the practical everyday psychology of the Stoic school. By being strict on yourself in the early stages, you'll find it a lot easier to build Stoic resilience and self-discipline into your daily life.

Broaden Your Affection: Let's say you have a favorite coffee mug or an old and well-loved fishing pole or any other object you're especially fond of. People often get emotionally attached to favorite objects like this. As a beginner at Stoicism, you would probably be upset if you dropped your favorite mug and shattered it or if your beloved old fishing pole fell off the back of the boat and disappeared into the lake. Every time you pick up this well-loved object of yours, ask yourself what it is and answer honestly. It's only a coffee mug, and there are many other good coffee mugs out there. It's only a fishing pole, and there are plenty of good fishing poles. Instead of focusing on the specific object, try to broaden your feeling of affection to include the broader category the object belongs to. Epictetus suggests doing this even when you kiss your child goodnight or put your arms around your spouse, telling yourself that you are simply kissing or hugging a human being. As with anything else in Stoicism, it's probably wiser to start small rather than trying to take this advice to such an extreme setting right away.

These Things Happen: Sometimes, we understand things better from a little distance. We usually don't overreact to a situation unless it affects us personally because we find it easier to see the situation for what it really is. For example, if you were over at a friend's house and your friend's child spilled a glass of milk, you certainly wouldn't get irritated over such a minor incident. What would you say? Probably, "these things happen" or something of the sort because it is true that these things will happen. What happens when your child spills a glass of milk? If you're like a lot of other parents, you'd probably get irritated at your child's carelessness and say something like, "I've asked you a thousand times to be more careful." Is there any real difference between the two situations? There is—only the amount of distance between you and the source of stress. Practice telling yourself, "these things happen," even in situations where you're directly involved. If you can make this a habit, you'll start to find it easier to look at your own life the way you would look at someone's else's life, with just enough distance to remember that "these things happen."

Don't Chatter: The phrase "strong but silent" is a cliché and might remind you of a John Wayne type of character: stoic on the outside, whatever emotional turmoil might lie beneath. In the practice of Stoicism, "appropriate" actions are considered good training for "perfect" actions, so being stoic on the outside can help you become Stoic on the inside over time. Epictetus advises his students not to talk too much, saying only a few words and only when necessary. He doesn't go as far as to forbid conversation, but he does tell his students to avoid any of the "common topics" that tend to get people worked up emotionally. Most importantly, Epictetus says to avoid talking about other people and their actions. Don't praise them, don't blame them, and don't compare them to each other. Why? Some actions are praiseworthy, and some are not. Some actions deserve blame or embarrassment. People can easily be compared to each other in various ways—this one is smarter, that one stronger. It doesn't matter. Blaming, praising, and comparing all have the same problem. They divert your mind from its proper focus, which is always your own actions and never anything external. According to Epictetus, your silence during an inappropriate conversation may even bring it to a halt, stopping people from repeating harmful gossip and innuendo.

Control Your Laughter: Epictetus says not to laugh too often and not to laugh too long or too loudly. This might seem a little harsh, and Epictetus is probably the harshest of all the Stoics. It's not that there's anything wrong with laughter, though. After all, joy is one of the "good feelings" even a Sage can safely indulge. The reminder to control your laughter is a training exercise to keep your mind as focused and self-disciplined as a Stoic's should be. In addition, laughter is frequently cruel in some way. Imagine a coworker telling a funny story, the theme of which is the stupidity and incompetence of one of your other coworkers. Is that a story you can laugh at safely or a situation where you should remain silent? If you can control your laughter in that situation, you will also avoid the mistake of criticizing others. Like the speech of a Stoic, the laughter of a Stoic should be relatively infrequent.

Avoid Vulgar Language: It would probably take a Sage not to swear in some circumstances, such as hitting your thumb with a hammer. Epictetus knows this, but he still asks his students not to swear, if possible, and to keep it to a bare minimum, if swearing simply cannot be avoided. Yelling out something colorful when you hit your thumb with a hammer is more like an "impression," an involuntary reaction rather than a choice. Swearing casually or excessively is more like "assent," the acceptance of false judgment. Like all the other exercises in this chapter, you should think of this more as a training exercise than an absolute rule. Having said that, it's hard to imagine a Stoic swearing often or loudly.

Avoid Vulgar Entertainment: Again, it's not that any particular type of entertainment is good or bad. In the Stoic view, good and bad are never found in external things but only in your reaction to them. From rock shows to professional wrestling to a horror movie, the things people do to pass the time are all indifferent. However, popular forms of entertainment usually try to provoke intense emotions. The better the entertainment is, the more emotion it provokes. For training purposes, it's usually better for a Stoic to avoid popular (and especially vulgar) entertainment. If you happen to find yourself at such an event, you can still use it as an opportunity for Stoic practice. First, try not to get caught up in the emotions around you. If everyone else is shouting and stamping their feet, avoid doing the same. Second, avoid any display of superiority or condescension. Try to stay calm and unaffected, without seeming to disapprove of everyone else. If you can avoid being swept away on the tide of emotion, you'll find it easier to do so in your daily life as well. It should be noted that Stoic philosopher Seneca wrote plays, including at least eight tragedies. A Stoic should avoid any entertainment based on the crude manipulation of extreme emotion, but that doesn't mean you can't enjoy a good movie or a good book.

Avoid Luxury: To teach yourself how to do without, Epictetus advises living a life of intentional minimalism. Don't buy the fanciest cut of steak or that bottle of expensive single malt Scotch. Don't wear designer clothes. Don't buy or build the most luxurious house.

Epictetus actually says to confine yourself to what is merely useful, never going beyond bare necessity. The much wealthier Seneca wasn't anywhere near as harsh. He only advocated living such a minimalist lifestyle a few days out of every month. Both approaches are training methods rather than absolute rules. Minimalism, like luxury and refinement, is an external thing. However, having the bare necessities won't cause you to become addicted to luxury, but living a luxurious lifestyle will probably make it much harder for you to deal with hardship if it ever becomes necessary. To achieve Stoic independence from external things, it can be helpful to reduce your need for such things before you have to.

Be Careful About Sex: Sexuality is such a powerful biological instinct that most people would find it difficult to abstain from sex completely. If you aren't in a committed long-term relationship, Epictetus says it's better to abstain if possible, but he acknowledges that it won't be possible for everyone. If you don't think you can abstain, it's best to be careful. Don't overindulge, and don't participate in anything harmful or exploitative. While holding yourself to the highest standard that you can manage, avoid giving the impression that you look down on people who do things differently than you. In general, Stoicism teaches us to be stern with ourselves but easy on others. Making a point of your high standard of behavior is just as contrary to Stoicism as having no standard of behavior. This is a difficult line to walk since people who notice that you do things differently will often assume that you're looking down on them even if you haven't given them any reason to think so. While holding your actions to a high standard, try to project an easygoing and nonjudgmental attitude about the actions of others. That way, you can avoid both extremes.

"May the Best Man Win": This saying exemplifies the Stoic attitude to athletic competition. The way Epictetus phrases it is slightly different. He says that you should wish the winner to be whoever ends up winning. Strictly speaking, the better man could lose due to a fluke, and a Stoic still wouldn't get upset about that because it would still be something beyond the control of the will. Still, "may the best man win" is close enough for our purposes and will keep you from getting too worked up about the outcome of any particular game. A lot of people get wildly emotional about their favorite team—elated when their team wins, despondent when it loses. Your team's win-loss record is not under your control, so like any other external thing, it is indifferent to a Stoic. That doesn't mean you can't have a "preferred team" as a practicing Stoic. Remember, indifferent things can still be preferred or not preferred. Even if you do have a preferred team, your underlying attitude should still be "let the best man win." If you watch the game with that mentality, you won't be disappointed by the results, no matter what they are.

What Would Epictetus Do?: Epictetus himself doesn't say "what would Epictetus do." He tells us to imagine what Socrates or Zeno would do, especially when meeting an important person. It's hard to imagine the fearless Socrates or the noble-minded Zeno behaving without dignity and self-respect in front of anyone alive—not even a powerful and dangerous ruler. For the modern Stoic, asking, "what would Epictetus do?" is an equivalent exercise. If you have to meet the CEO of the company or perhaps a politician, don't say or do anything you couldn't imagine Epictetus doing in the same situation. This exercise can help you avoid doing or saying anything you might regret later on, no matter how nervous you feel about meeting the big man in person. This exercise can also be helpful if you happen to meet a celebrity for some reason.

Don't Tell Too Many War Stories: Even if you've lived a life filled with action and excitement, other people may not want to hear about it as often as you think. The ups and downs of life can be entertaining, and often, the worst experiences make the wildest anecdotes. At social events, such as parties, people often tell stories about their adventures. For a Stoic in training, the risk is that you will become too focused on the opinions and reactions of your audience. Do you want them to laugh and think you're funny, to be amazed at your courage, or to envy your exciting experiences? In all those situations, your mental focus is on something outside your control. Some of the most entertaining anecdotes involve bad decisions and their consequences. Are people laughing with you, or are they laughing at you? As with swearing and sex, Epictetus doesn't ban anecdotes completely, but he does say not to tell stories about your adventures very frequently. In addition, if someone else is telling an anecdote about something reprehensible, you should make it clear, through your response, that you don't want to hear that kind of story.

Be a Fatalist: The ancient Stoics were fatalists, believing much of life to be predestined by the gods. To Marcus Aurelius or Seneca, complaining too loudly about your life is like telling the gods they made a mistake. It won't fix whatever problems you have, but it will tend to alienate you from the gods. Of course, you don't have to believe everything is predestined or worry about angering God to practice Stoicism. Even if events are not predestined, you can still accept whatever is beyond your control. Still, thinking of events as decrees of Fate can be a useful exercise because it reduces the tendency to wish things were different when you can't do anything about it. Epictetus suggests using a line by the Greek playwright Euripides as a maxim:

"I follow cheerfully; and, did I not,
Wicked and wretched, I must follow still."

When something can't be changed, you just have to live with it. If you accept it cheerfully, you won't feel bad about it. If you don't accept it, you'll have to go through it anyway, but you'll be wretched. As Euripides says, accepting fate without complaint is a sign of genuine wisdom.

Memento Mori: The Latin phrase *memento mori* means "remember death." It's not meant to be grim, but a simple reminder that our time is limited. We all have to die, and none of us knows when our time will end. In one of his letters, Seneca talks about checking the time. Some people always want to know the time of day, but never give any more thought to how much time they have left to live. If you knew that you had exactly ten more years, how would you spend your remaining time? What if it was only ten more months or ten more hours or ten more minutes? If you weren't sure how much more money you had left in your checking account, you'd be wary of spending a single dollar for fear of an overdraft. According to Seneca, we'd all be much more conscious of how we spent our time if we understood the fact that life could end at any moment. By reminding yourself constantly of the reality of death, you can focus your mind on what is truly essential and make every minute count.

Negative Visualization: The phrase "negative visualization" probably sounds like the exact opposite of all the feel-good, positive-thinking advice you've ever heard. As counterintuitive as it might be, negative visualization is a foundational technique of Stoic daily practice. It's not intended to make you sad or anxious but to inoculate you against sadness and anxiety—like a mental vaccine. The basic idea behind negative visualization is a simple one. Instead of telling yourself that bad things won't happen, you tell yourself that they *will* happen but that you can handle it.

It's a good idea to start small, rather than trying to tackle the big anxieties of life right away. Before you do anything, you should visualize the irritating things that usually happen. For example, if you're going to the movies, you should imagine people talking or a tall man sitting in front of you without taking off his hat. Remind yourself that you aren't just planning to go to the movies; you are going to the movies while keeping your mind calm and settled. If people do end up talking during the movie or blocking your view, you should find it easier not to get irritated because you prepared yourself ahead of time.

Once you have some experience at negative visualization, start applying it to things that are more serious than trivial irritations. For example, if you want to ask your boss to approve a major project, tell yourself that she won't agree to meet you. If she does agree to meet you, she'll cancel or reschedule the meeting. If the meeting happens, she'll ignore or disagree with everything you say. If she approves the project, she'll insist on changing your plans and micromanaging the process. By picturing all the things that would usually stress you out in that kind of situation, you can avoid getting stressed out when and if they actually happen. Paradoxically, this can even reduce the odds that any of these things will end up happening. Your boss is much more likely to trust your judgment if you come across as calm and self-controlled than if you seem anxious and needy.

As an experienced practitioner of negative visualization, you should deliberately visualize the worst things that can possibly happen. Illness, homelessness, injury, death—anything that scares you should be the subject of a negative visualization exercise. By imagining frightening things in the safety of your mind, you can reduce your fear reaction until it disappears, leaving you free from that particular anxiety.

Review Your Actions: Just before you go to sleep, think back over everything you said and did. Which actions were appropriate and which actions were inappropriate? Do you have anything to be proud of, any moment in which you lived as a Stoic? For example, did you succeed in remaining calm and dignified in a stressful situation or self-disciplined in the face of temptation? Allow yourself to feel proud and happy because you're making progress toward genuine freedom. Is there any moment you regret, any action unworthy of a Stoic? For instance, did you lose your temper or indulge in something that wasn't good for you? Admit your fault, and fill yourself with a firm determination to do better tomorrow. Some Stoics find journaling to be the most effective way to do this exercise because you can go back and review your journal later to track your progress. The *Meditations* of Marcus Aurelius began as a diary, showing that this exercise was known to the ancient Stoics. Your diary probably won't have readers a thousand years from now, but it can still help you practice Stoicism daily. As you gain experience, you should find your ability to live philosophically improve over time. When you look back at earlier entries and see how far you've come, you'll gain confidence and a sense of quiet happiness at how much Stoicism has already done for you.

Chapter 9: The Stoic Leader

"Where a man can live, there he can also live well. But he must live in a palace; well then, he can also live well in a palace."

- Marcus Aurelius

Stoicism has long been considered the ideal philosophy for leaders, perhaps because of its association with powerful rulers like Marcus Aurelius, Frederick the Great, and George Washington. Modern political leaders like Wen Jiabao, business leaders like Jack Dorsey, and even athletic leaders like Michael Lombardi still base their leadership styles on Stoic principles.

There's a bit of a paradox here because "command" is one of the things we have no control over. Rank and authority are external things, and all external things are indifferent to a Stoic. A practicing Stoic may even find a leadership position to be a little bit awkward because it makes the practice of Stoicism much harder. For example, Marcus Aurelius didn't seem to have been particularly interested in the position of emperor and was tempted to resent all the demands it placed on him. He didn't use this as an excuse to neglect his responsibilities. Instead, he used his responsibilities as an opportunity to practice Stoicism.

In his *Meditations*, the emperor compared the imperial court to a stepmother and philosophy to a mother. A good man would never neglect his stepmother and would always treat her with respect, but his warmth and affection for his birth mother would always be stronger. The Stoic leader governs well but never loves power for its own sake.

The Nine Rules of Stoic Leadership

In his *Meditations*, Marcus Aurelius wrote a list of nine rules for the Stoic leader. These rules emphasize the importance of not losing your temper with the mistakes of your subordinates, an important consideration for an emperor with the power of life and death. Even though few modern leaders have so much power, the same principles still apply. Before making a decision that can affect someone else's life, consider these nine points.

1. Think of yourself as a bull leading a herd of cows or a ram leading a flock of sheep. The role of the bull or the ram is to protect and guide, knowing that all the members of the group exist to help each other and that none could thrive without the others.

2. Ask yourself what kind of people your subordinates are. What are they like at work? What are they like at home? What are they like among their friends? What opinions do they hold, and what do they seem to take pride in?

3. Whenever a subordinate does well, be pleased with them. Whenever they do poorly, remember that they don't do so intentionally but because of their own ignorance of the best way to act.

4. Always remember your faults and bad habits before judging others. Even if you do have better habits, remember the poor motives that often underlie them. For instance, if you work longer hours because you want other people to see you as hard-working, then your actions are still only appropriate rather than perfect.

5. Consider the circumstances before making a decision, and remember that you may not have complete information. Sometimes, it seems like a mistake has been made only because the full context is not yet known.

6. If you're so angry that you just can't let it go, remind yourself that nothing lasts forever and that all this will seem trivial and not worth worrying about once enough times has passed.

7. Remind yourself that the actions of another can never hurt you. The only thing that can ever hurt you is your own opinion.

8. Remind yourself that far more trouble is caused by anger than by the things that usually make people angry.

9. Correct the errors of your subordinates gently and with patience, with the goal of teaching rather than punishing.

The Advice of the Emperor

The nine rules are intended to protect you from the consequences of a hasty judgment based on a momentary flash of anger, but there's a lot more to leadership than just being patient with the people who work for you. Gems of useful leadership advice are scattered throughout the *Meditations*, which is not surprising because Marcus Aurelius was responsible for leading an entire empire. Here are some of the Stoic emperor's tips for leaders.

Lead by Mentoring: The entire first book of the *Meditations* is a list of the people the emperor learned from and what they taught him. He thanks his grandfather for teaching him to control his temper, his father for teaching him modesty, his mother for teaching him to live simply, and a series of tutors for teaching him the principles of the Stoic life. Marcus Aurelius often reminds himself to think of leadership as a teaching opportunity, guiding others on the right path in life through a combination of patient instruction and his own example. Your goal as a leader should be to mentor all those who work under your authority.

Consider the Whole: Always remember the whole and your part in it. That means considering the whole organization, your role within the organization, and what responsibilities flow from that role. The responsibilities of the role may sometimes go against your inclinations, but as the leader, you still need to fulfill your role. Never think of yourself as merely an individual but always as an individual embedded in a network of relationships. No matter what might be going on, no one can prevent you from fulfilling the responsibilities associated with your role to the best of your ability.

Appreciate Imperfection: Marcus Aurelius uses the example of a loaf of bread that has split in baking. This is something bakers usually try to avoid, but to a customer buying a loaf of bread, there is still something appetizing about the sight of a split loaf. Imperfections can be appealing, especially if you know how to put them to good use. A timid person can be useful in a position requiring meticulous attention to detail. A reckless person might spot opportunities other people would miss. Leading people effectively is often a matter of making good use of their imperfections.

Embrace Change: Change is inevitable, yet people fear and resist it all too often. Marcus Aurelius compares the flow of events in human life to the flow of water. On one level, nothing changes, but on another level, change is all there is. That's because there is nothing about change that prevents an underlying continuity. There is nothing harmful about change, though our fear of change often causes us harm. If you encounter any resistance to a planned change, remind the people who work for you that nothing happens without change. You can't take a shower without changing the water from one form to another, and you can't eat dinner without changing the food. If you find yourself resisting change, remind yourself that change is the one precondition for every single thing that happens. Pushing back against change is like pushing back against life.

Don't Be Too Suspicious: In one passage of his *Meditations*, the emperor cautions himself against being too suspicious. Rather than worrying about what other people are doing or what their real motives might be, he reminds himself to concentrate on his actions and motivations. The alternative is paranoia, an easy and very dangerous temptation for any leader. The emperor's goal was to be able to answer the question "what are you thinking?" immediately and directly, without needing to leave any of his thoughts unsaid. This is only possible if you guard your thoughts just as carefully as you guard your actions.

Be Willing to Change Your Opinions: In a position of leadership, it's easy to interpret any disagreement as a direct challenge to your authority. Even if you don't take disagreement personally, it can still be hard to let go of your own opinions. Marcus Aurelius reminds us that it is not a sign of weakness or lack of authority to change your opinions when presented with a convincing argument. A leader who can never change his mind seems brittle and fragile. Only yes-men and sycophants will voluntarily follow a leader like that. If you show yourself willing to be convinced, your subordinates won't be afraid to present you with new ideas or point out possible issues before they develop into serious problems.

Keep a Sense of Proportion: Don't give anything more attention than it really deserves, especially the petty dramas of office politics. It can help to imagine a scene from the past, such as your own organization before you joined it or some other organization a hundred years ago. People were flirting, flattering, plotting against each other, stealing from the company, having birthday parties, getting promoted, taking vacations, and so on. Technology changes, but people don't. Don't give too much attention to things that will never change.

Get Up and Get at It: The sound of the alarm clock is often unwelcome, but most people have little choice except to drag themselves out of bed and get to work. For a Roman emperor like Marcus Aurelius, the temptation to remain in bed must have been a strong one. After all, who's going to tell Caesar to stop lying around and get to work? To motivate himself on mornings like these, the emperor had several mental tricks. One was to remind himself that he was a member of society and that it was time to get up and contribute to society. Another trick was to think about the ants and the birds that get up and do their work without needing anyone to nag at them. He also reminded himself of artists and people obsessed with a personal project and who will often go without sufficient sleep just to get a chance to work. Whatever it takes to get you moving, don't let the relative privilege of your position make you lazy and unfocused. Get up and get started, thinking of your work as an opportunity to practice your philosophy.

Don't Keep Track of Favors: Some people will never do a good deed for anyone without considering it a debt. Treating every human relationship as a *quid pro quo* is a losing strategy because not everyone will pay you back as you think you deserve, and you will be repeatedly disappointed. Marcus Aurelius compares a good leader to a grapevine, which naturally produces new grapes every season without ever expecting a reward for it. Help your subordinates at every opportunity without calling attention to yourself or expecting anything in return for your benevolence. Those who understand and appreciate what you've done for them will be loyal in return, while those who do not would have been ungrateful anyway. You'll get all the benefits of the *quid pro quo* approach without any of the drawbacks.

Look in the Mirror: Constantly ask yourself what kind of personality or character you currently have—what kind of "soul," as Marcus Aurelius says. Looking in the mirror may not be easy, but you can't hope to improve unless you're brutally honest in your self-assessment. Do you have the character of an inspiring leader, or would some other word describe you more accurately? The emperor mentions several possibilities—a child, a wild beast, a tyrant, and a weakling. If you can't describe yourself as a strong leader with a straight face, that's a sign that you need to change something.

Live Well Wherever You Are: Unlike the followers of Aristotle, the Stoics never considered wealth or power a prerequisite for living well. As Marcus Aurelius says, a good person can live well anywhere. If this is the case, then it follows that a good person can live well "in a palace." The possession of wealth and power is not a prerequisite for wisdom or happiness, but neither is it an impediment to them. In a position of authority, it's important to remind yourself that you are deeply responsible for the well-being of everyone who works for you. Since you happen to be in the palace, you must do your best to govern well.

Don't Take Things Personally: All your subordinates will make mistakes, but a few will do something that goes far beyond a mere mistake. Actions such as embezzlement or sexual misconduct reveal deep flaws in a person's character and also expose the company to legal risk. When you discover misconduct, take firm action, but don't take it personally. It's irrational to expect a person of poor character not to do bad things, so misconduct is simply evidence that the person responsible has that type of character. You can take whatever action is needed without letting it shake you, knowing that they simply did what a person of that type will always do.

Obstacles are Indifferent: Rivals and competitors will always exist, and sometimes, they will prevent you from achieving your goals. For example, a rival on the board of directors might sabotage your project, or a competing company may land the contract you were going for. The Stoic should always think of other people as fellow members of the human community to be helped wherever possible, except when they interfere with your goals and become obstacles. In this case, Marcus Aurelius says you should think of them the same way you would think of the weather or a dangerous animal. You might not be able to go outside in the pouring rain, but you'd think of the rain as a mere obstacle, not an enemy. You might not walk down a street with a fierce dog on it, but you wouldn't see the dog as a personal foe. To a Stoic, all obstacles are equally indifferent, including people who stand in the way.

No Harm to the Hive: When you're part of a group or a community with a common goal and purpose, you identify yourself with that goal and stop thinking in a self-centered way. As Marcus Aurelius says, nothing is harmful to the bee unless it harms the hive. Whenever you're frustrated in your role as a leader, ask yourself whether the situation that's frustrating you harms the whole organization or is just a hassle. Unless it prevents the organization from achieving its goals, it's probably not worth so much stress in the first place.

If It Needs to be Done, Do it Right: Anything that ever needs to be done can be done well or poorly, including the things that are most laborious, unpleasant, or uncomfortable. Whatever you have to do to fulfill your responsibilities as a leader, ask yourself what the best way to do that thing is, and make sure to do it that way. For example, many companies have fallen victim to attacks by hackers because they failed to download and install critical updates soon enough. Patching software is a thankless task and frequently slows down the whole company until the task is done. Some business leaders prefer to put off such a bothersome task, patching infrequently or inconsistently. Their desire to keep the company running smoothly is understandable. That doesn't change the fact that patching is necessary and procrastinating is dangerous. Getting taken over by hackers typically costs far, far more than updating software regularly. If it has to be done, there's no advantage in waiting just because it's a hassle. By doing things the right way no matter how inconvenient, you can save yourself a lot more trouble down the road.

The Stain of Power: Marcus Aurelius compares habits of the mind to a bright dye, easy to be stained by and hard to wash out. In ancient Rome, purple was a color reserved for emperors. Although he was the emperor himself, Marcus Aurelius expressed concern in his diary about being "stained" by the dye of Caesar. A leadership position is a grave responsibility, and the power that comes with the position can easily change how you think if you don't watch out for it. Once you start to think of yourself as the person who *should* be in charge rather than the person who *happens* to be in charge, it will be hard to keep your equilibrium. Stoic leadership is servant leadership. The goal is the general welfare, not your personal power.

According to Marcus Aurelius, a Stoic leader should be, "simple, good, pure, serious, free from affectation, a friend of justice, kind, affectionate, and strenuous in all proper acts." From the moment you assume a leadership role, you should be on guard not to let any of the "imperial purple" spill on you and stain your thoughts. The craving for power is an especially hard dye to wash out.

Stand in a High Place: This technique is often called "The View From Above," and comes from Plato originally. To get a big-picture view, imagine yourself standing in a high place, such as a mountaintop or a balcony on a very tall building. Look down from above and see everything all at once in your mind's eye. Watch the factories where your products are made, the container ships carrying your company's products across the ocean, or the accountant driving home to the suburbs when the day is done. Try to imagine how everything is interconnected and how all the different parts affect each other on a daily basis. The more often you do this exercise, the better you will understand how your organization works, and what it needs from you as a leader.

Understand the Past to Understand the Future: Look back on the history of your organization and of similar organizations before your own. If you're a coach, study the history of the great teams. What made them so successful, and what led them to stop winning championships, eventually? If you lead a company, research the history of your industry. What companies used to dominate and no longer do? What changes happened and why? Whatever happened before will happen again, always in new forms but always the same. The purpose of studying history is to recognize patterns so that you can use those patterns appropriately and strategically in your role as a leader.

Actions Show Principles: When you're considering someone for a position of responsibility, the most important point is to know what principles they live by. You can't always find this out by asking questions because most people will tell you what they think you want to hear. The best way to find out their real opinions is to observe their actions because they'll give away what they believe. Do they do things the right way when they think you're watching but slack off when they think you aren't paying attention? Do they try to sacrifice others for their advantage or claim credit for work that is not their own? The things people do in life show what they think, no matter what principles they claim to hold. To discover their real principles, observe their actions. The secrets of human character are in what we do, not what we say.

Let All Your Actions Be Social: As a leader of others, your role in society is for the good of the whole. According to Marcus Aurelius, all your actions should serve a social purpose, and you should think of any purely personal action as something that tears your life into two pieces. Rather than compartmentalizing our lives into the personal and the public as so many people do, the emperor advises us to keep an undivided focus on general welfare. Of course, this doesn't mean to neglect your family and friendships to focus solely on work. Our actions toward friends and family members are also social and part of the leader's social responsibility.

To sum up the Stoic approach to leadership, the Stoic leader is a mentor and public servant who always puts the well-being of the whole above any narrow concerns. The Stoic leader is patient and forgiving and looks for ways to use imperfections as advantages wherever possible but hires and promotes based on character. The Stoic leader seeks the View From Above, always looking for the big picture. The Stoic leader is always willing to change when appropriate and never loves power for its own sake.

Conclusion

Thank you for making it to the end of *Stoicism: The Manual of Ancient Stoic Philosophy as a Way of Modern Life*. Let's hope it was informative and able to provide you with all of the tools you need to achieve your goals whatever they may be.

In this book, you've learned about the history of Stoicism and the great Stoic thinkers whose ideas have survived to the present day. You've learned the basics of the Stoic practice, including the four passions to avoid and the three good feelings to cultivate. You've learned how to respond to first impressions with Stoic pragmatism and critical thinking, how to cultivate more resilience and self-discipline, and how to manage emotional turmoil with the Stoic mindset. You've learned how Stoicism has inspired some of history's greatest leaders, how it has influenced modern psychology, and how you can apply it in your daily life.

The next step is to get started with the four most important and helpful Stoic habits:

- Practice being mindful of your actions and judgments.
- Question your first impressions.
- Remember that you are part of a whole.
- Imagine what can go wrong and see yourself overcoming it.

With these four habits as a starting point, you can go on to cultivate the serenity and untroubled happiness of the Stoic way of life. The most important to remember is a simple one: focus on what is under your control and disregard everything that isn't.

www.ingramcontent.com/pod-product-compliance
Lightning Source LLC
Chambersburg PA
CBHW071619080526
44588CB00010B/1198